MTTC

English Practice Questions

Mometrix

TEST PREPARATION

DEAR FUTURE EXAM SUCCESS STORY

First of all, **THANK YOU** for purchasing Mometrix study materials!

Second, congratulations! You are one of the few determined test-takers who are committed to doing whatever it takes to excel on your exam. **You have come to the right place.** We developed these practice tests with one goal in mind: to deliver you the best possible approximation of the questions you will see on test day.

Standardized testing is one of the biggest obstacles on your road to success, which only increases the importance of doing well in the high-pressure, high-stakes environment of test day. Your results on this test could have a significant impact on your future, and these practice tests will give you the repetitions you need to build your familiarity and confidence with the test content and format to help you achieve your full potential on test day.

Your success is our success

We would love to hear from you! If you would like to share the story of your exam success or if you have any questions or comments in regard to our products, please contact us at **800-673-8175** or **support@mometrix.com**.

Thanks again for your business and we wish you continued success!

Sincerely,
The Mometrix Test Preparation Team

Printed in the United States of America

Table of Contents

Practice Test #1

Refer to the following for questions 1–5:

In the United States, where we have more land than people, it is not at all difficult for persons in good health to make money. In this comparatively new field there are so many avenues of success open, so many vocations which are not crowded, that any person of either sex who is willing, at least for the time being, to engage in any respectable occupation that offers, may find lucrative employment.

Those who really desire to attain an independence, have only to set their minds upon it, and adopt the proper means, as they do in regard to any other object which they wish to accomplish, and the thing is easily done. But however easy it may be found to make money, I have no doubt many of my hearers will agree it is the most difficult thing in the world to keep it. The road to wealth is, as Dr. Franklin truly says, "as plain as the road to the mill." It consists simply in expending less than we earn; that seems to be a very simple problem. Mr. Micawber, one of those happy creations of the genial Dickens, puts the case in a strong light when he says that to have annual income of twenty pounds, per annum, and spend twenty pounds and sixpence, is to be the most miserable of men; whereas, to have an income of only twenty pounds, and spend but nineteen pounds and sixpence, is to be the happiest of mortals.

Many of my hearers may say, "we understand this; this is economy, and we know economy is wealth; we know we can't eat our cake and keep it also." Yet I beg to say that perhaps more cases of failure arise from mistakes on this point than almost any other. The fact is, many people think they understand economy when they really do not.

Excerpt from *The Art of Money-Getting* by P.T. Barnum

1. Who is the most likely audience for this passage?

a. Economists
b. General readers
c. Teachers
d. Philanthropists

2. Which word best describes the author's attitude towards those who believe they understand money?

a. Supportive
b. Incriminating
c. Excessive
d. Patronizing

3. Which of the following statements best expresses the main idea of the passage?

a. Getting a job is easier now than it ever has been before.
b. Earning money is much less difficult than managing it properly.
c. Dr. Franklin advocated getting a job in a mill.
d. Spending money is the greatest temptation in the world.

4. What would this author's attitude likely be to a person unable to find employment?

a. Descriptive
b. Conciliatory
c. Ingenuous
d. Incredulous

5. What is the best definition of *economy* as it is used in this passage?

a. Exchange of money, goods, and services
b. Delegation of household affairs
c. Efficient money management
d. Less expensive

Refer to the following for questions 6–11:

In the United States, the foreign language requirement for high school graduation is decided at the state level. This means the requirement varies, with some states deciding to forego a foreign language requirement altogether (www.ncssfl.org). It is necessary that these states reconsider their position and amend their requirements to reflect compulsory completion of a course of one or more foreign languages. Studying a foreign language has become increasingly important for the global economy. As technology continues to make international business relations increasingly easy, people need to keep up by increasing their communication capabilities. High school graduates with foreign language credits have been shown to have an increased college acceptance rate. In addition, students who have mastered more than one language typically find themselves in greater demand when they reach the job market. Students who did not study a foreign language often find themselves unable to obtain a job at all.

6. What is the main idea of this passage?

a. Studying a foreign language will help graduating students find jobs after high school.
b. Studying a foreign language should be a mandatory requirement for high school graduation.
c. Studying a foreign language helps students gain an understanding of other cultures.
d. Studying a foreign language is essential if a student hopes to get into college.

7. Which of the following statements represents the best summary of the claims made in this passage?

a. Studying a foreign language is important if you want to graduate from high school and get a job.
b. Studying a foreign language is important for the global economy because of the technological advances that have been made in international communications.
c. Studying a foreign language is important for the global economy, college acceptance rates, and becoming a sought-after candidate in the job market.
d. Studying a foreign language is important for college acceptance rates and obtaining a job after college.

8. Which of the following statements represents an exaggerated claim in support of the argument presented in this passage?

a. In the United States, the foreign language requirement for high school graduation is decided at the state level.
b. Studying a foreign language has become increasingly important for the global economy.
c. High school graduates with foreign language credits have been shown to have an increased college acceptance rate.
d. Students who did not study a foreign language often find themselves unable to obtain a job at all.

9. Which of the following would be a useful source of information to determine the validity of the argument presented in this passage?

a. A survey of high school students' preferences with regard to foreign language requirements
b. A comparison of the correlation between a second language introduced at home and subsequent college acceptance rates
c. A survey that asks parents to select the foreign language they would like their children to study in high school
d. A comparison of the correlation between high school students' study of a foreign language and subsequent college acceptance rates

10. Which of the following would be the best concluding statement for this passage?

a. States should consider how important foreign languages are for the global economy when making their policies regarding foreign language requirements for graduation from high school.
b. Policies regarding a foreign language requirement for graduation from high school should take into account the importance of foreign languages for the global economy and the correlation between foreign languages and increased college acceptance rates and employment opportunities.
c. High school graduation requirements should include a foreign language class because of the influence knowledge of a second language has on college acceptance rates.
d. Policies regarding a foreign language requirement for graduation from high school should take into account how difficult it is to obtain a job in today's economy for those who do not have knowledge of more than one language.

11. Based on this passage, the author would most likely agree with which of the following?

a. Learning a foreign language is only for fun, and it should be up to the individual to decide whether or not they wish to learn one.
b. Learning a foreign language should be a basic requirement for all students because studies have shown that it improves the local economy.
c. Learning a foreign language is an unreasonable expectation for the government to place upon students since most people find no need to speak more than one language.
d. Learning a foreign language needs to be compulsory for all students in the United States.

Refer to the following for questions 12–15:

> It was the best of times, it was the worst of times, it was the age of wisdom, it was the age of foolishness, it was the epoch of belief, it was the epoch of incredulity, it was the season of Light, it was the season of Darkness, it was the spring of hope, it was the winter of despair, we had everything before us, we had nothing before us, we were all going direct to heaven, we were all going direct the other way – in short, the period was so far like the present period, that some of its noisiest authorities insisted on its being received, for good or for evil, in the superlative degree of comparison only.
>
> Excerpted from *A Tale of Two Cities* by Charles Dickens (1859)

12. Which of the following ideas did Dickens want to convey in this introduction?

a. The extreme good and bad described were only imagined by "authorities."
b. Everything could seem to be best or worst depending on the individual.
c. The past era described was indistinguishable from the present one.
d. The readers' present era and this past era both had good and bad.

13. Of the following statements, which accurately describes textual evidence of Dickens's techniques and their effects?

a. The rhythm and anaphora reinforce the idea of equal and opposing forces.
b. The presentation of multiple pairs of opposites introduces a paradox motif.
c. The author's use of anastrophe and rhythm emphasizes contrasting opposites.
d. The author uses repetition to slow the pacing of the story.

14. Among the following, which pair is most figurative in meaning?

a. Wisdom and foolishness
b. Belief and incredulity
c. Light and darkness
d. Hope and despair

15. From reading only this introductory paragraph, what can readers infer about the rest of this novel?

a. The story will likely include equal amounts of good and bad.
b. The story will likely focus more on bad than good.
c. The story will likely explain how good and bad are really the same.
d. The story will likely show how good can come from bad.

Refer to the following for questions 16–17:

> Edward Bulwer-Lytton's 1830 novel *Paul Clifford* opens, "It was a dark and stormy night; the rain fell in torrents—except at occasional intervals, when it was checked by a violent gust of wind which swept up the streets...rattling along the housetops,

and fiercely agitating the scanty flame of the lamps that struggled against the darkness."

16. The author's establishment of the setting contributes most to which of the following literary elements?

a. Plot
b. Tone
c. Mood
d. Conflict

17. Which part of speech do the most descriptive words in the passage belong to?

a. Verbs
b. Nouns
c. Adverbs
d. Adjectives

Refer to the following for questions 18–20:

Mamzelle Aurélie possessed a good strong figure, ruddy cheeks, hair that was changing from brown to gray, and a determined eye. She wore a man's hat about the farm, and an old blue army overcoat when it was cold, and sometimes top-boots.

Mamzelle Aurélie had never thought of marrying. She had never been in love. At the age of twenty she had received a proposal, which she had promptly declined, and at the age of fifty she had not yet lived to regret it.

She was quite alone in the world, except for her dog Ponto, and the negroes who lived in her cabins and worked her crops, and the fowls, a few cows, a couple of mules, her gun (with which she shot chicken-hawks), and her religion.

Excerpted from "Regret" by Kate Chopin, 1894

18. Which type of characterization does the author give in the first paragraph?

a. Direct
b. Indirect
c. Direct and indirect
d. No characterization, just description

19. In the second paragraph, what type of characterization does the author primarily use?

a. Direct
b. Indirect
c. Neither direct nor indirect
d. An equal mix of direct and indirect

20. This passage's third paragraph consists of which of these?

a. Description without any added characterization
b. Direct characterization throughout the paragraph
c. Mostly description with some indirect characterization
d. Direct and indirect characterization in equal parts

Refer to the following for questions 21–23:

Use the following stanzas from Alfred, Lord Tennyson's "The Charge of the Light Brigade"

Half a league, half a league,
Half a league onward,
All in the valley of Death
Rode the six hundred.
"Forward, the Light Brigade!
Charge for the guns!" he said.
Into the valley of Death
Rode the six hundred.

"Forward, the Light Brigade!"
Was there a man dismayed?
Not though the soldier knew
Someone had blundered.
Theirs not to make reply,
Theirs not to reason why,
Theirs but to do and die.
Into the valley of Death
Rode the six hundred.

21. What is the *first* literary device with which Tennyson opens the first stanza above?

a. Metaphor
b. Repetition
c. Hyperbole
d. Imagery

22. What effect(s) does the poet accomplish with the sound of the first two lines?

a. He creates a marching rhythm.
b. He makes the sense of distance seem lessened.
c. He establishes a weary mood.
d. Choices A and C are correct, but not Choice B.

23. How do the form and word choice of lines 13–15 in the second stanza contribute to their meaning?

a. They reflect the complexity of the battle through their variety.
b. They reflect the men's heroic humility and honesty through their simplicity.
c. They reflect the treacherous nature of war through their irregularity.
d. They reflect the tedium of the soldier's life through their monotony.

24. Suppose you want to know whether a used car you are looking at is a good vehicle to buy, and the salesperson calls attention to its beautiful paint job. In assessing the relevance of this argument, which of the following applies most?

a. The paint job is more relevant than the condition of the transmission.
b. The paint job is less relevant than the fact that the car's frame is bent.
c. The paint job is more relevant than how well the vehicle's engine runs.
d. The paint job is less relevant than anything because this is not relevant at all.

25. When writing an essay, which is the best way to address multiple main points?

a. Write a separate paragraph for each point, including the point's supporting evidence and its relation to the thesis.
b. Introduce each point in one paragraph, support it in another, and relate it to the thesis in another.
c. Cover all main points, supporting evidence, and their connections with thesis in one long paragraph.
d. Address each main point in a logical order using any number of paragraphs necessary for readability.

26. When writing an essay, which of the following attributes belongs in the introduction?

a. Getting the reader's attention
b. Developing the thesis statement
c. Giving examples of the thesis idea
d. Giving the reader a sense of closure

27. Which of the following is most accurate regarding the sequence of steps a reader should take to evaluate arguments in an informational text?

a. Readers should find supporting premises and only look for the conclusion once these are understood.
b. Readers should first identify an argument's conclusion and then identify the premises supporting it.
c. Readers should note an argument's conclusion and supporting premises in the order they are presented.
d. Readers should try to paraphrase premises to clarify them, not to make them fit with the conclusion.

28. Someone argues, "But if you legalize this drug, all drugs will be legalized." In rhetoric, this is an example of which type of logical fallacy?

a. Straw man
b. Red herring
c. Slippery slope
d. *Post hoc ergo propter hoc*

29. Of the following, which statement is true about instruction in the alphabetic principle?

a. Letter-sound relationships with the highest utility should be the earliest ones introduced.
b. The instruction of letter-sound correspondences should always be done in word context.
c. Letter-sound relationship practice times should only be assigned apart from other lessons.
d. Letter-sound relationship practice should focus on new relationships, not go over old ones.

30. "This treatise developed from an initial idea like a plant develops from a seed." The preceding sentence is an example of which literary device and argument method?

a. Analogy
b. Allegory
c. Allusion
d. Antithesis

31. Which of the following sentences is an example of the fallacy of irrelevance?

a. There are exceptions to all general statements.
b. Please pass me; my parents will be upset if I fail.
c. He is guilty; there is no evidence that he is innocent.
d. Have you stopped cheating on your assignments?

32. Which statement is accurate regarding guidelines for searching when conducting a literature review for writing a research paper?

a. Too many references indicate the research question is not narrow enough.
b. Too few references indicate the area of investigation is not specific enough.
c. No references at all indicate the topic and research question must be invalid.
d. Writers should search for references before determining the topic of their research paper.

33. Which of the following statements correctly describes research findings regarding effective writing instruction techniques?

a. Teacher modeling and think-alouds are effective.
b. Providing students with scaffolding can slow learning.
c. Exposing students to the processes of writing is sufficient.
d. Implicit and embedded instruction is better than explicit instruction.

34. Based on research evidence, what do experts recommend to effectively instruct students in writing strategies?

a. Teachers should demonstrate strategies and then assign independent student practice.
b. Teachers should explain strategies and let students practice them without any models.
c. Teachers should model strategies, then guide practice, then give independent practice.
d. Teachers should first give students guided practice in strategies and then model them.

35. When evaluating writing strategies, what does research find about effective instruction of middle school students?

a. Explicit instruction is best for teaching specific tasks, such as writing argumentative essays.
b. Explicit instruction is better for teaching brainstorming, editing, or other general processes.
c. Explicit instruction is necessary to teach specific, general, planning, and compositional tasks.
d. Explicit instruction is more important to teach revising and editing than planning for writing.

36. Which of these accurately reflects research findings about effective writing instruction methods?

a. Procedural strategies like mnemonics, graphic organizers, outlines, and checklists aren't very useful.
b. Studies show teaching cognitive strategies is helpful only to students of certain ages and ability levels.
c. Students need explicit instruction, modeling, think-alouds, and scaffolding to learn how to write well.
d. Teaching self-regulation improves only student awareness of their writing strengths and weaknesses.

37. According to literacy experts, what is true about student writing?

a. The primary purpose of student writing is expressing their ideas, thoughts, and emotions.
b. The primary purpose of student writing is persuading their readers to agree with and believe them.
c. Improving student reading skills improves their writing skills, but not the other way around.
d. Improving student writing skills as well as their reading skills improves their learning ability.

38. The phrase "pretty as a picture" is best described as a:

a. Metaphor
b. Simile
c. Synecdoche
d. Paradox

39. The smallest functional unit of speech is a:

a. Word
b. Phoneme
c. Syllable
d. Letter

40. Which of the following choices represents the smallest unit of language that possesses semantic meaning?

a. Morpheme
b. Grapheme
c. Phoneme
d. Word stem

41. A history teacher discusses the structure of nonfiction texts by explaining the text structures of comparison and contrast, cause and effect, problem and solution, and chronological order. Which text structure do the following chapter titles from *A Textbook of the History of Architecture* represent?

CHAPTER I: PRIMITIVE AND PREHISTORIC ARCHITECTURE
CHAPTER X: .EARLY CHRISTIAN ARCHITECTURE
CHAPTER XIII: EARLY MEDIAEVAL ARCHITECTURE IN ITALY AND FRANCE
CHAPTER XX: EARLY RENAISSANCE ARCHITECTURE IN ITALY
CHAPTER XXVII: ARCHITECTURE IN THE UNITED STATES

a. comparison and contrast
b. cause and effect
c. chronological order
d. problem and solution

42. The teacher and her students brainstorm a list of talents, skills, and specialized knowledge belonging to members of the class. Some of the items on the list include how to make a soufflé, how to juggle, and how to teach a dog to do tricks. One student knows a great deal about spiders, and another knows about motorcycles. The teacher asks the students to each write an essay about something they are good at or know a great deal about. What kind of essay is she asking the students to produce?

a. Cause and effect
b. Compare/contrast
c. Expository
d. Argumentative

43. Which text(s) are likely to foster the greatest enthusiasm for reading and literature among students?

a. Free choice of reading texts, provided that students complete class assignments, projects, and discussions
b. An all-in-one textbook that includes all reading material for the year, study guides, and sample test questions
c. A variety of texts, including books, magazines, newspapers, stories from oral traditions, poetry, music, and films
d. A small selection of current best-selling books for children, some of which the children may already have read and liked

44. Mark Twain famously included several distinctive versions of Southern US English in *Adventures of Huckleberry Finn* (1884). Which of the following are these versions of English examples of?

a. Jargon
b. Slang
c. Dialect
d. Accent

45. What is the main role of literature, as described in the passage?

> Throughout history, literature has served as a mirror to society, reflecting its joys, struggles, and complexities. Novels like *To Kill a Mockingbird* by Harper Lee shed light on issues of racial injustice, while George Orwell's *1984* explores the dangers of totalitarianism. These literary works continue to provide valuable insights into the human condition.

a. To entertain readers with fictional stories
b. To provide a glimpse into historical events
c. To reflect societal issues and human experiences
d. To promote the study of totalitarianism

46. Which of these is an example of attributes to seek in good children's literature?

a. Stable story characters who do not change
b. Books featuring overtly moralistic themes
c. Concise summaries of race/gender types
d. Original yet believable plot constructions

47. Which of these is most accurate about the function of dialogue in fictional literature?

a. Dialogue can serve to advance the plot but not develop characters.
b. Dialogue can serve to illuminate themes and meanings and redirect plots.
c. Dialogue can serve to break up exposition and slow the pace of the story.
d. Dialogue can serve to reproduce real speech instead of adding drama.

48. Among the following, which element is found exclusively in only one genre of literature?

a. Plot
b. Characters
c. Stage directions
d. Rhymed/free verse

49. Which of the following literary elements are most likely to be found in both fictional narratives and nonfictional informational text?

a. The writing style of the author
b. Labeled diagrams and photos
c. Excitement and drama
d. Themes and plots

50. In research fields, what does *literature* mean?

a. All the written works in a language
b. The profession of a writer or author
c. All existing research on a subject
d. Any kind of printed materials

51. Which choice is the most correct statement about mood and tone in literature?

a. Mood and tone are synonyms referring to the emotional atmosphere of the work.
b. Mood is the emotion evoked in the reader by the work; tone is the author's emotion.
c. Mood is the emotion expressed by a work's author; tone is the emotion evoked in the reader by the work.
d. Mood is established by authors using different literary techniques than those used in creating tone.

52. An eighth-grade class will be watching a mystery film in English class over the next two days. Throughout the story, the camera will often focus on objects or clothing that are colored bright red. These objects are always related to clues that lead the character toward solving the mystery. What literary device is the students' teacher planning to introduce in this context?

a. Media deconstruction
b. Color imagery
c. Alliteration
d. Symbolism

53. Of the following, which is NOT common in both satire and realism?

a. Irony
b. Serious tone
c. Exaggeration
d. Vernacular dialogue

54. In comparing and contrasting the sonnet and the ballad as subgenres of the literary genre of poetry, which of these do both forms have in common?

a. They both have five main kinds.
b. They both often express love.
c. They both began with music.
d. They both have equal meter.

55. Within the literary genre of poetry, which function is more characteristic of the ballad than the sonnet?

a. Relating a story about human interactions
b. Demonstrating skill with writing the poem
c. Being included as part of theatrical plays
d. Satirizing romantic, political, and social issues

56. In an informational text, which of these is most likely to make use of the others?

a. Irony
b. Satire
c. Overstatement
d. Understatement

57. Which of the following genres takes an opinion and defends it?

a. Essays
b. Biographies
c. Memoirs
d. Informational texts

58. Which of the following genres is most important for children just beginning to become readers in grades K, 1, and 2?

a. Alphabet books, wordless picture books, and easy-to-read books
b. Legends and tall tales
c. Biographies and informational books
d. Chapter books and fantasy books

59. Which of the following is NOT a goal of children's literature?

a. Focus on choices, morals, and values.
b. Instruct students through entertaining stories.
c. Promote an interest in reading itself.
d. Instruct students in the sciences, such as mathematics and biology.

60. Which of the following is true about the author's point of view in an informational text?

a. Readers can easily identify the author's point of view because informational texts include it as a main idea.
b. Readers often must infer the author's point of view because informational authors tend not to explicitly state it.
c. Readers may see the author's point of view equally well for neutral, balanced, and opinionated positions.
d. Readers who must analyze a text to identify the author's point of view can assume the text is poorly written.

61. A teacher plans to use the drawing below to explain story elements. Each point on the line represents an element of the story. Which choice matches the point on the chart with the smiling face above it?

a. Rising Action
b. Exposition
c. Resolution
d. Climax

62. What is the author's purpose in using this opening paragraph?

In the opening lines of J.D. Salinger's novel *The Catcher in the Rye*, Holden Caulfield, the protagonist, expresses his disdain for "phony" people and institutions. He criticizes his peers for their superficiality and hypocrisy, describing them as "living in a museum." He expresses his preference for the "real" world, even if it's messy and imperfect.

a. To introduce the main character and his perspective
b. To set the tone of the novel as lighthearted and optimistic
c. To provide a summary of the plot of the novel
d. To persuade readers to agree with Holden's views

63. Which of the following aspects of poetic form is characteristic of haiku?

a. A 5-7-5 syllable pattern
b. An ABA rhyme scheme
c. Perfectly regular meter
d. Lengthy epic narratives

64. Two mothers of young children write their observations about parenting. Writer A publishes her writing daily for a wide reading audience. Writer B also writes daily, but privately. Which two forms of writing best identify their activities?

a. Blog; journal
b. Journal; letters
c. Letters; essays
d. Essays; speeches

65. Which of these is a term that is NOT typically used about a literary dramatic work?

a. Act
b. Scene
c. Stanza
d. Chapter

66. Abi, a fifth-grader, is reading aloud to his teacher during one-on-one reading time. His teacher uses this time to evaluate ongoing fluency and comprehension skills. Following today's reading, Abi's teacher determines that he needs practice with words that begin with digraphs. Which of the following sets of words would most likely be part of this assignment?

a. Chicken, Shells, That
b. Were, Frame, Click
c. Sponge, Think, Blank
d. Packed, Blistered, Smoothed

67. Which of the following instructional strategies would help students recognize the text structures of comparison and contrast or cause and effect in a history textbook?

a. defining the historical events occurring in a certain time period
b. showing students how to recognize signal words such as "similar to" or "instead of," which show these text structures
c. providing a timeline of the period of history being discussed
d. discussing the maps provided throughout the textbook

68. Commercials for a mobile service provider frequently reiterate the question, "Can you hear me now?" Which technique of persuasion does this best represent?

a. Pathos
b. Slogan use
c. Bandwagon
d. Testimonial

69. Which of the following best demonstrates writing appropriately for a specific task, purpose, and audience?

a. Using jargon in a book report that will be read aloud to classmates
b. Using simple language when describing a new procedure to expert colleagues
c. Using vivid, entertaining language when writing a story for young students
d. Using humor to request new privileges from one's parents

70. Which of these sets of factors would most greatly affect a student's reading comprehension in class and on tests?

a. Oral language development, written language development and eating a healthy breakfast.
b. Word analysis skills, sight word knowledge and ability to monitor understanding.
c. Vocabulary development, sight word knowledge and reference skills.
d. Prior knowledge, good classroom participation and academic performance in other subjects.

71. Which of the following MOST accurately summarizes the relationship between reading fluency and reading comprehension?

a. As students develop greater reading comprehension, their reading fluency also improves.
b. When students develop greater reading fluency, their reading comprehension improves.
c. The relationship between reading fluency and reading comprehension is a reciprocal one.
d. Reading fluency and reading comprehension are two separate, mainly unrelated skill sets.

72. Jamie's teacher presents her class with a unit about Mexico that includes information about the customs, geography, language, and cuisine of the country. While the teacher is showing pictures of a traditional Mexican festival, Jamie raises his hand to share some of the object-names he remembers from his family's annual trip to Mexico. This scenario is an example of:

a. Paradigm emergence
b. Prior knowledge activation
c. Chunking
d. Immersion theory

73. Which of the following choices is NOT an element of metacognition?

a. A reader's awareness of themselves as a learner
b. A reader's understanding of a variety of reading strategies
c. A reader who is conscious about remembering what has been read
d. A reader who can read with prosody

74. Which instructional activity is the best example of the research-based strategy of activating students' prior knowledge before reading?

a. Before students read a text, the teacher instructs them in relevant background information.
b. Before and after they read a text, the teacher has students make a KWL chart on its subject.
c. After students have read a text, the teacher asks them what they know about the subject.
d. The teacher asks students to express their opinions and reactions on a topic after reading.

75. Which statement accurately reflects a principle regarding self-questioning techniques for increasing student reading comprehension?

a. Asking only what kinds of "expert questions" fit the text's subject matter
b. Asking only those questions that the text raises for the individual student
c. Asking how each text portion relates to chapter main ideas is unnecessary
d. Asking how the text information fits with what the student already knows

76. After reading Shakespeare's Romeo and Juliet in class, students watch the most recent Hollywood film version, starring Leonardo DiCaprio. Their teacher leads a class discussion after the film. Which of the following essay topics would be most helpful in challenging students to analyze how visual media affects their perceptions of a piece of literature?

a. Discuss your favorite character in the film version of Romeo and Juliet, and give at least three reasons to back up your opinion.
b. Which version of Romeo and Juliet did you like better, and why?
c. Compare the film with the play and point out at least four instances in which portions of the play were left out of the film version.
d. Describe the setting of the film and discuss why you think the film's director chose to portray the play in modern times.

77. Which of the following choices would be the least effective example of an integrated curriculum that includes language arts instruction?

a. Ms. Smith, a language teacher, confers with Mr. Langston, a history and social studies teacher. Ms. Smith shows Mr. Langston how to model previewing and predicting skills before he introduces a new unit or assignment so that the students build their comprehension skills while reading for information.
b. A science teacher recognizes that the students are having difficulty retaining information from their science textbooks when test time arrives. She creates a study guide with leading questions designed to help jog the students' memory about important concepts before the test.
c. Ms. Shannon, an art teacher, plans a field trip to see the latest exhibit featuring a symbolic artist. A language teacher at her school joins the students at the museum to lead a discussion about the function of symbols and their meanings, as well as different methods of interpreting shared symbols in a society.
d. A 1st-grade teacher uses children's books that introduce mathematical skills. For example, she reads a book weekly that tells a story about children preparing for a picnic, adding and subtracting items they need for the trip along the way. She encourages the children to solve the math questions along with her during the story.

78. Some experts maintain that teaching reading comprehension entails not only the application of skills but also the process of actively constructing meaning. They describe this process as interactive, strategic, and adaptable. Which of the following descriptions best applies to the interactive aspect of this process?

a. The process involves the text, the reader, and the context in which reading occurs.
b. The process involves readers using a variety of strategies in constructing meaning.
c. The process involves readers changing their strategies to read different text types.
d. The process involves changing strategies according to different reasons for reading.

79. Which of the following reading assignments would be most appropriate as a context for teaching students how to preview information to improve comprehension?

a. A written version of a popular movie that most of the students have seen outside of class.
b. A reading assignment from the students' science class that they will be tested on next month.
c. A novel the students read in English class last year.
d. A set of poems that will be studied next month during Poetry Week.

80. Which of the following is the best use of technology in a language arts classroom?

a. Providing laptops to students to achieve more effective note-taking, access to word processing programs, and access to the internet
b. Encouraging the use of slide shows or similar programs to support lectures and oral presentations, as well as to organize pertinent class concepts
c. Incorporating a computer-based "language lab" in which students can listen to texts and engage in interactive word-study and comprehension activities
d. Whenever possible, watching film interpretations based on texts studied in class

81. Which of the following reading comprehension strategies is *most* applicable to differentiating between homonyms without knowing their exact spellings?

a. Pictures
b. Phonics
c. Context
d. Grammar

82. When reading an expository text, the reader would most appropriately draw which kinds of inferences?

a. Cause-and-effect and/or problem-solution
b. What events occurred and what people did
c. What the author wants readers to believe
d. Ideas that support the author's message

83. Which of these accurately reflects influences on media choices for giving presentations?

a. Combining more than one type of media is advisable.
b. Experts find it more effective to limit presentations to one medium.
c. Presenters should not let their budgets influence their choice.
d. The length of communication will not affect the media.

84. If a student has an assignment to speak before the whole class on a given topic and include a visual aid, which of the following technological tools would be most appropriate?

a. A slide show
b. A poster
c. A blog
d. A wiki

85. Which of the following is most accurate about the relationship between the physics of thinking and speaking as these inform classroom instruction in listening actively?

a. Because thinking outpaces speech, students' minds wander, so listening is less effective than reading.
b. The disparity between speaking and thinking speeds is conducive to active listening via summarizing.
c. The process of listening is an inherently social interaction; the process of learning is not equally social.
d. The process of learning is essentially a reciprocal one, but the process of listening is not as reciprocal.

86. Mr. Callas is introducing a unit on oral traditions from around the world. He wants his seventh-grade students to gain a better understanding of the relationship between written text and oral language, as well as increase their multi-cultural understanding. Which of the following assignments would be the most relevant?

a. "Read Chapter 12 on Oral Traditions and complete the end-of-chapter review."
b. "Select a poem or song from a culture around the world and recite it for the class."
c. "Conduct a poll of twenty fellow students, asking about their family's country of origin. Present a graph or diagram of your results in class."
d. "Choose a country to research and write a first-person narrative about a typical day in the life of one of its citizens. The narratives will be read in class."

87. Mrs. Canas has had a parent offer to visit her fifth-grade class and provide a sign language seminar. The parent is fluent in American Sign Language and would like to offer her skills to benefit the students. Mrs. Canas thinks the seminar will be very interesting and provide a unique way to hone her students' listening and expressive skills. Which choice identifies another language skill set that would indirectly benefit from this seminar?

a. Students' understanding of how visual messages, including body language, facial expression, and signs inform verbal communication and ideas.
b. Students' fine motor skills and hand-eye coordination.
c. Students' respect for other cultures, specifically the non-hearing community.
d. Students' ability to communicate with other peers and adults in their community.

88. For supporting language acquisition in ESL/ELL students, what is most accurate about research-based instructional practices?

a. Teachers should only state directions verbally to give ELLs English decoding practice.
b. Teachers should encourage ESL students to respond rapidly to get them up to speed.
c. Teachers should use idioms without explanations to familiarize ELL students to these.
d. Teachers should give ELL students models and examples of what they expect in tasks.

89. Young children tend to learn vocabulary more effectively when under certain levels of demand. Which of the following best represents an appropriate use of demand for activities made to support acquisition of new vocabulary words?

a. Teachers alternate between low-demand and high-demand questions.
b. Teachers employ new vocabulary in clear contexts, but do not provide direct support.
c. Teachers restrict their questions to those with low complexity until students demonstrate mastery.
d. Teachers move from low-demand question to high-demand ones.

90. Which of the following instructional techniques would be most appropriate for building and monitoring students' listening skills?

a. Read a story, poem, or other piece of literature to them each day before beginning class.
b. Give pop quizzes on the day's lessons at the end of class.
c. Preview concepts that will be introduced in class and then allow the students to answer recall-based questions verbally at the end of class.
d. Pay close attention to the students' answers on tests when they relate to classroom discussions.

91. Which component of oral language development involves the social rules for using language?

a. The pragmatic component
b. The phonological component
c. The semantic component
d. The syntactic component

92. Which of the following exercises would be the most appropriate tool for helping students evaluate the effectiveness of their own spoken messages?

a. Discuss written and oral assignments in class before completing them. Once the assignments are completed, the teacher meets individually with each student to discuss the content and effectiveness of each student's work.
b. Instruct students to present oral reports in class, which are then "graded" by classmates. A score of 1-10 is assigned based on students' perception of the reports' clarity. The students' average scores determine the effectiveness of each report.
c. Ask each student to prepare an oral report and a content quiz that highlights the report's main idea. The student then uses classmates' scores on the reviews to determine the report's effectiveness.
d. Put students into groups of three. Two students complete a role-playing assignment based on prompts provided by the teacher. The third student gives constructive feedback on how the other two can refine and clarify their speech.

93. Which of the following statements most accurately compares the components of speeches and the components of essays?

a. Speeches and essays have similar introductions.
b. Speeches provide supporting evidence in greater detail than essays do.
c. The conclusion of a speech must be more forceful and engaging than the conclusion of an essay.
d. Speeches may include greetings, mentions of honored guests, and thanks, but essays should not include these elements.

94. Each week, a teacher asks one student to bring in a recording of his favorite song and a written version of the lyrics. The students listen to the song and receive a copy of the lyrics. They discuss these words as either one large group or in small groups. What are these students probably learning from this exercise?

a. Students are learning about the lives of their peers indirectly by listening to each student's favorite song; they can begin to understand each other by the meaning behind the song lyrics.
b. Students are learning that they are very diverse in many ways: they have different musical tastes and prefer many different styles of music and expression.
c. Students are learning that it is very difficult to communicate freely when bound by various musical traits such as rhyming, rhythm, and phrasing.
d. Students are learning that literacy skills do not just pertain to schoolwork. These skills allow students to understand and communicate meanings through a variety of ways, including music and lyrics.

95. When establishing ground rules for collaborative student discussions, which of these should teachers include?

a. Teachers should encourage students by allowing them to jump in with comments at any time.
b. Teachers should encourage talkative students to hold forth to take pressure off of shyer ones.
c. Teachers should include in student discussions ground rules that students must not engage in cross talk.
d. Teachers should include rules against verbal abuse, but physical abuse is too unlikely for rules.

96. To provide accommodations for ELL students, which of these should teachers do in vocabulary and reading instruction?

a. Teach ELL students vocabulary in isolation.
b. Teach ELL students vocabulary in context.
c. Teach ELL students vocabulary in volume.
d. Teach ELL students reading by their speech levels.

97. What statement is correct regarding effective teacher techniques for classroom discussions?

a. Teachers making comments instead of asking questions encourages creativity in student responses.
b. When some students dominate discussion, teachers engage others with more challenging questions.
c. To meet learning goals, teachers can redirect off-subject discussion by restating topics and questions.
d. A checklist based on the class attendance roll is not the best way to assess all students' participation.

98. A teacher is working with a group of English language learners. She asks them to take two pieces of paper. At the top of the first paper, they are to write *SAME*, and at the top of the other, *DIFFERENT*. Each child will consider what his native country and the United States have in common, and what distinct features each country possesses. The children are using which method in organizing their ideas?

a. Hunt and peck
b. Consider and persuade
c. Evaluate and contrast
d. Compare and contrast

99. A classroom teacher observes that a new ELL student consistently omits the /h/ sound in words. Of these, what is the first factor the teacher should consider?

a. The student may have an articulation disorder.
b. The student may be a native Spanish speaker.
c. The student may need a hearing assessment.
d. The student may have a respiratory problem.

100. Which of the following factors affects ELL students' English-language literacy development?

a. A Chinese student's L1 is not written alphabetically like English is.
b. A Spanish student's L1 is more phonetically regular than English is.
c. Neither one of these has any effects on L2 literacy development.
d. Both factors affect L2 literacy development but in different ways.

Answer Key and Explanations for Test #1

1. B: This passage is clearly intended for a non-expert adult readership. It uses language that general readers can understand, and uses a reference to a Charles Dickens character that readers of the time might be familiar with (Mr. Micawber in the novel *David Copperfield*) to illustrate its point. Economists certainly understand economy better than Barnum (the author) does and so would not need this explanation, and there is nothing in the passage to indicate that Barnum is specifically writing for teachers or philanthropists.

2. D: The author suggests that many people who believe that they understand how to become wealthy in fact do not, and that he knows better than they do. The word *patronizing* means condescending, or talking down to someone. The author implies that he understands economy better than most of his readers despite it being so simple that everyone should understand it.

3. B: The author asserts that earning money is easy, but what often challenges people is managing money. This is the main idea of the passage. Choice B says that earning money is less difficult than managing money, so it is correct. Getting a job and the temptation to spend money are both mentioned in the passage as details. However, neither of these are the main idea, so choices A and D are both incorrect. The quote from Franklin does not advocate for working at a mill and does not summarize the main idea, so choice C is also incorrect.

4. D: The author seems to believe that there are plenty of lucrative jobs for everyone, so he or she would doubt that a person really could not find employment. This makes choice D the best choice, as *incredulous* means to struggle to believe something. *Descriptive* means describing, *conciliatory* means satisfying or appeasing, and *ingenuous* means innocent. None of these terms describe the attitude of the author, so choices A, B, and C are incorrect.

5. C: In this passage, the author is speaking of money management on a personal or household level. In this context, *economy* refers to efficient money management, so choice C is correct. While this definition of *economy* is relevant to households, it is not related to delegation within a household, making choice B incorrect. *Economy* in the context of the exchange of money, goods, and services is more applicable beyond personal or household finances, so choice A is incorrect. This passage uses *economy* to describe wise money management, not simply goods that are less expensive than others, so choice D is incorrect.

6. B: The passage argues that high schools should require that students study a foreign language and gives reasons to support this argument. Choice B accurately describes the main idea of the passage. The passage does say that studying a foreign language is helpful for college acceptance and finding a job, but neither of these points are the main idea of the passage. They are both supporting details. The passage does not say that studying a foreign language will help students gain an understanding of other cultures.

7. C: The passage includes claims that studying a foreign language is helpful for participating in the global economy, being accepted into college, and being a desirable candidate for various jobs. These points are summarized in choice C, making it the best summary of the passage. The passage argues that studying a foreign language should be mandatory, but it does not claim that studying a foreign language is currently essential to high school graduation, so choice A is incorrect. Choices B and D represent claims made in the passage but do not include all of the claims made.

8. D: Although students may find knowledge of a foreign language helpful for obtaining a job, it is clearly an exaggeration to claim that students who did not study a foreign language are unemployable. Choice A simply lists a fact that can be verified, so it cannot be an exaggeration. Choices B and C include statements that the importance of knowing a foreign language and the acceptance rates for students who have studied a foreign language have increased. These statements simply describe the direction of a trend, so while they can be incorrect, they cannot be exaggerations.

9. D: Choice D can confirm the author's claim that high school graduates who have studied a foreign language are more likely to be accepted to college, so it is correct. Choices A and C would provide information regarding the opinions of students and parents but not actual evidence regarding the influence of studying a foreign language on future success. Choice B specifies a second language taught at home, whereas the passage focuses specifically on a foreign language taught in high school.

10. B: Choice B emphasizes the passage's argument and includes a summary of the main supporting details used to defend it. This makes choice B the best conclusion. Choices A, C, and D each emphasize the passage's main argument, but each one only mentions one supporting detail. These are not effective conclusions, so they are incorrect.

11. D: The author makes their position clear that they believe learning a foreign language should be required of all students in the country, not just for those in the states that choose to have that requirement.

12. D: Charles Dickens uses a series of opposites to convey the idea that the period described involves extremes of positive and negative. He also likens the period to the present time in that certain institutions are interested in people believing in these extremes. He does not say that the extremes are only imagined (A), that personal subjectivity dictates whether a given extreme is seen as good or bad (B), or that this past era and the present era are identical (C).

13. A: The even rhythm and ample use of anaphora emphasize the concept of equal, opposing forces. Anaphora is the repetition of a phrase to start consecutive clauses, creating a parallel. The presentation of multiple opposites introduces a theme of doubles that highlights conflict rather than contradiction, so choice B is not correct. Choice C is not correct because it mentions anastrophe, which reverses adjective-noun order to noun-adjective, such as in the phrase "ocean blue." Anaphora is relevant here, not anastrophe. Repetition of an entire sentence can be used to slow the pacing in a story, but the repetition here is limited to the beginnings of the clauses. The ending of each clause is different, so there is no slowing effect, making choice D incorrect.

14. C: In the sense that Charles Dickens uses them here, *light* and *darkness* do not mean physical illumination or its absence. Their meanings are instead figurative, with *light* referring to good, knowledge, happiness, hope, etc., and *darkness* referring to bad, ignorance, unhappiness, despair, etc. The other three choices all use words whose most literal meaning is applicable, so these pairs are not figurative in meaning.

15. A: Because of the balancing of opposites in the introduction, readers can infer that this balance will likely be present throughout the story. There is no reason to expect it will focus more on bad, as choice B states. Though the introduction mentions that the "superlative degree of comparison" is "for good or for evil," it does not suggest that there is really no difference between good and bad, so choice C is incorrect. Choice D is incorrect because, even though the story may show how good can come from bad, there is no reason to view this possibility as particularly likely from reading the passage.

16. C: Though the first clause of this sentence has been widely maligned, ridiculed, parodied, praised, imitated, and even made the basis of literary contests for both bad and good writing, it and the rest of the sentence do establish the setting such that it contributes greatly to mood, i.e., the emotions it evokes in readers. It does not contribute to plot (A) because it includes no actions or events yet. It does not contribute to tone (B), which reflects the attitude of the author rather than evoking an attitude in the reader. It does not contribute to conflict (D) in the same way it does not contribute to plot.

17. D: The arguably most descriptive words in this sentence are adjectives: dark, stormy, violent, scanty. Bulwer-Lytton also used verbs (A), i.e., fell, was checked, swept, rattling, agitating, struggled; although the last four of these are descriptive, they are arguably not as descriptive as the adjectives. He used some descriptive nouns (B) as well: night, rain, gust, wind, darkness; yet these are still not as evocative as the adjectives. Of adverbs (C), "fiercely" is certainly descriptive, but it is the only one.

18. A: By describing and commenting on the character's appearance, the author provides direct characterization. Mamzelle Aurélie's strong figure suggests a strong character, her ruddy cheeks imply vigorous health and personality, her determined eye implies a determined spirit, and even her dress suggests that she is independent. Thus, Chopin uses Mamzelle Aurélie's physical appearance to tell readers what Mamzelle Aurélie is like. Simply describing the character's thoughts, dialogue, or actions so that readers may interpret them would be indirect characterization. This paragraph gives an example of direct characterization only, so choices B, C, and D are incorrect.

19. A: Chopin primarily uses direct characterization in this paragraph by telling readers that the character had never considered marriage, never been in love, and had not yet lived to regret it. This directly tells readers about this aspect of her character. Indirect (B) characterization would instead show readers about it through the character's actions, thoughts, and/or words, as well as those of other characters. Chopin mentions that the character had promptly declined a proposal, which could be a form of indirect characterization. However, the majority of the paragraph features direct characterization. Since choice A is correct and choice B is incorrect, choices C and D are also incorrect.

20. C: This paragraph includes mainly description, but there is also a small amount of indirect characterization; thus, choice A is incorrect. While the phrase "she was quite alone in the world" does provide direct characterization, the majority of the paragraph is either description or indirect characterization. Thus, choices B and D are incorrect. Her having a dog, being religious, and shooting chicken-hawks herself with her gun are elements of indirect characterization. The rest of the paragraph is description establishing setting and situation more than character—i.e., she owned a farm and employed farmhands.

21. B: The first device Tennyson opens with is repetition, repeating the phrase "Half a league" three times. He uses a metaphor (A) second when he refers to "the valley of Death," implicitly comparing death to a valley. He does not use hyperbole (C), which is extreme exaggeration for effect, or imagery (D), which is a description that evokes mental images—visual, auditory, and/or of other senses—as his first device. While "the valley of Death" is a poetic image as well as a metaphor, this is used second, not first.

22. D: The sound of the first two lines creates a rhythm reminiscent of soldiers marching, which is their subject, by repeating dactylic (/◡◡) and trochaic (/◡) beats. The phrase "half a league" refers to how far they must march (approximately 1.5 miles). The repetition of this phrase does not minimize the distance (B) but emphasizes it as well as establishes the mood of the soldiers' weariness (C).

23. B: These lines do not involve a lot of variety (A) but rather, contain very simple, short words—only two with two syllables, the rest with just one—as well as a consistent rhythm. Also, all three lines begin with the same word (*Theirs*), and all three end with rhyming words (*reply, why, die*). This simplicity reflects the meaning that the soldiers do not talk back to their superiors and do not conjecture about rationales for the battle, but simply do their jobs, which often includes dying. These lines are not irregular (C) in rhyme, meter, word choice, word length, etc. Though regular, they are not monotonous (D); in fact, they are some of the most famous, oft-quoted lines from the poem.

24. B: When assessing the relevance of any argument, it is important to remember that relevance is a matter of degree, not an either/or or yes/no proposition. In this example, the salesperson's argument for buying the car because of its great paint job is *less* relevant than the transmission's condition (A), which is more important in a good vehicle. The paint job is less relevant than a bent frame (B), which negatively affects the car's function and value; or how well the engine runs (C), which affects functioning far more than the paint job. However, the paint job is not completely irrelevant (D): most customers want good-looking used cars.

25. A: Using one paragraph to introduce one main point is advised, present evidence supporting that point, and explain how this point relates to the thesis. Each additional main point, its supporting evidence, and its relation to the thesis should occupy a separate paragraph. This method is summarized in choice A. Choice B is incorrect because main points should not be separated from their supporting evidence or the explanations of how they relate to the thesis. Choice C is incorrect because including all main points, their accompanying evidence, and their relation to the thesis in one long paragraph would provide almost no structure, making the essay more difficult to read and understand. Similarly, dividing topics into as many paragraphs as necessary, as is described in Choice D, can lead to an unnecessarily long and unfocused essay.

26. A: The introduction of an essay should get the reader's attention, engage the reader's interest, state and integrate the main thesis within it, and give an overview of the essay's organization or structure (for example, by summarizing the main point and supporting evidence). Developing the thesis statement and giving examples of the idea in the thesis both belong in the body of the essay. Giving the reader a sense of closure belongs in the conclusion of the essay.

27. B: Readers should first identify the conclusion of an argument and then identify the premises the author gives to support that conclusion. Choice A is incorrect because the reader cannot find support premises without knowing the conclusion that needs to be supported. Choice C is incorrect because the author may present supporting premises before their argument's conclusion, but readers should first identify the conclusion when evaluating arguments. Choice D is incorrect because readers should try to paraphrase the premises to clarify them and show how they support the conclusion.

28. C: This is an example of a slippery slope argument that is a logical fallacy. The fallacious form of the slippery slope is essentially a non sequitur—it argues that one thing will cause other things without showing any cause-and-effect relationship between them. A straw man argument is a logical fallacy which, instead of refuting someone else's actual argument, refutes an exaggeration or caricature of it. A red herring is a piece of irrelevant information introduced to distract attention from the real issue. *Post hoc ergo propter hoc* is Latin for "After this, therefore because of this." It means arguing that one thing was caused by another that happened before it. This is a logical fallacy because, like correlation, chronological order does not equal causation.

29. A: While there is no consensus among experts as to any universal sequence of instruction for teaching the alphabetic principle through phonics instruction, they do agree that, to enable children to start reading words as soon as possible, the highest-utility relationships should be introduced earliest. For example, the letters *m, a, p, t,* and *s* are all used frequently, whereas the *x* in *box*, the sound of *ey* in *they*, and the letter *a* when pronounced as it is in *want* have lower-utility letter-sound correspondences. Important considerations for the alphabetic principle are to teach letter-sound correspondences in isolation, not in word contexts; to teach them explicitly; to give students opportunities to practice letter-sound relationships within their other daily lessons, not only separately; and to include cumulative reviews of relationships taught earlier along with new ones in practice opportunities.

30. A: This sentence is an analogy, which compares two concepts to establish a relationship, so choice A is correct. Analogy can enhance comprehension of a new concept via comparison to an older or more familiar concept. Allegory (B) uses symbolism to represent an abstract concept with a more concrete concept. Allusion (C) is a passing reference to a specific work, place, person, or event. For example, saying "Susan loves to help and care for other people so much that her friends call her Mother Teresa" is an allusion to a famous person that makes a point about how compassionate someone is. Antithesis (D) juxtaposes words, phrases, or sentences with opposite meanings, balancing these to add insight. A good example is Neil Armstrong's statement during the moon landing: "That's one small step for man, one giant leap for mankind."

31. B: Choice B is correct as it is an example of the fallacy of irrelevance; passing or failing is determined by course performance, so asking to be passed because of one's parents' reaction to failing is not a logical argument for getting a passing grade. The other choices are also examples of fallacies, but each one is different from the fallacy of irrelevance. Choice A uses the fallacy of inconsistency (i.e., self-contradiction). Saying there are exceptions to all general statements is itself a general statement. According to this statement itself, there must be an exception to it. In other words, there will be general statements that do not have exceptions, so the original statement cannot be true. Choice C is an example of a fallacy of insufficiency. We cannot assume something is true simply because there is no evidence that goes against it. Choice D is an example of the fallacy of inappropriate presumption. Asking someone if they have stopped cheating presumes that they have cheated in the past. The person being asked this question cannot answer "yes" or "no" without confirming that they have indeed cheated. The phrasing of the question reflects that the asker has inappropriately presumed "yes" and "no" are the only two possibilities, when it is actually possible that the person has not cheated.

32. A: When conducting a literature review, having too many references indicates the research question is too broad and needs narrowing, so choice A is correct. Having too few references indicates the area of investigation or the research question is too narrow and needs broadening, so choice B is incorrect. Having zero references, especially on cutting-edge topics, does not necessarily invalidate the topic or question, so choice C is incorrect. Choice D is incorrect because determining the topic of the research paper should be done prior to searching for references. This will help the writer determine which references are relevant and write a more focused paper.

33. A: Research into writing instruction has led to specific findings on the effectiveness of certain techniques. Teacher modeling and think-alouds have been found effective, so choice A is correct.

Providing students with temporary support (i.e., scaffolding) that can be gradually removed as their skills grow has not been shown to slow learning, so choice B is incorrect. Merely exposing students to writing processes has been found to be insufficient in teaching writing, so choice C is incorrect. Finally, explicit instruction has been found to be more effective than implicit or embedded instruction, so choice D is incorrect.

34. C: According to experts, research shows that teachers should explicitly teach their students writing strategies, including prewriting planning, composition, revision, and editing, by first modeling the strategies; then guiding students in practicing them; and then, once they have learned the strategies, letting students practice using them independently. They should not skip the guided practice step (A); students need assistance learning to apply demonstrated strategies before practicing on their own. Students learn better with, not without, teacher models (B), which must be presented before, not after, guided practice (D).

35. C: For teaching middle school students effective writing strategies, teachers need to give explicit instruction in specific tasks such as steps in writing argumentative essays (A) and in more general processes such as brainstorming, editing, etc. (B); teachers also should give explicit instruction in planning before writing and in revising and editing during writing (D). Explicit instruction is equally important to teach effective strategies for all of these.

36. C: Research studies have found that explicit instruction, teacher modeling, teacher think-alouds, and scaffolding (graduated, faded support) are all effective methods of writing instruction for all students. Research also shows that procedural strategies including mnemonic devices, graphic organizers, outlining, and checklists are helpful to students for planning and revision of writing. Studies find that teaching cognitive strategies helps students of all ages and ability levels, not just some. Teaching self-regulation not only improves student awareness of their writing strengths and weaknesses, but it also makes their writing work more strategic, empowers them to adapt the strategies they learn as they need, and increases their generalization and maintenance of the writing strategies they have learned.

37. D: Research into literacy development reveals that improvement in students' writing skills improves their overall learning ability, just as improvement in their reading skills also does. Expressing ideas, thoughts, and feelings (A) is *one* purpose of student writing, but not the only or main one. Another purpose is persuasion of the reader audience to agree with the writer's point of view and/or believe the writer's assertions—again, not the only or main purpose (B), but one of various purposes. Research also finds not only that improving student reading skills improves their writing, but *also* that, reciprocally, improving student writing skills improves their reading (C).

38. B: "Pretty as a picture" is a simile, which is a comparison of two unlike things using the words *like* or *as*. A metaphor is a similar comparison between two unlike things, but metaphors do not use the words *like* or *as*. Synecdoche is a phrase that uses a part to represent the whole of something. For instance, one might refer to "the crown" to refer to a royal family. Finally, a paradox is a statement that appears to contradict itself. All of these are considered figures of speech.

39. B: Phonemes comprise the syllables that make up words. While phonemes correspond to the letters of an alphabetic writing system, letters themselves are not units of speech.

40. A: A phoneme is a unit of language that represents the smallest unit of sound. For instance, the *k* in *kit* or the *ph* in *graph* both represent English phonemes. Graphemes are written phonemes and can be alphabetic letters, numbers, characters, punctuation marks, and so on. Neither phonemes nor graphemes have semantic meaning unless they are used as part of a larger unit of language, such as the morpheme. Morphemes can be roots, prefixes, and suffixes. The word *rechargeable* is comprised of three morphemes: *re*, *charge*, and *able*. Each component of this word has a meaning unto itself, but when combined with the others, each one is used to make a new word with a new meaning.

41. C: The titles are in chronological order. A is incorrect because the titles do not show comparison and contrast. B is incorrect because the titles do not show cause and effect. D is incorrect because the titles do not show problem and solution.

42. C: Expository essays are any type of essay in which the writer is providing meaningful information about a topic for the purpose of informing. Most of the topics listed in the example include informational tasks, explaining the process of doing something, such as baking or juggling. Expository essays can use various organizational schemes to help structure the information, such as by comparing and contrasting two things. An expository essay is different from an argumentative essay in that it is not trying to convince the reader of anything, but only trying to inform. Similarly, the purpose of a descriptive essay is to show detail, but not necessarily to inform about how something works.

43. C: Students can easily become bored or disinterested in reading if they are not exposed to a variety of reading texts. Also, reading can be overwhelming or frustrating for students who are still learning to read fluently or to comprehend what they read. By incorporating media, oral stories, and various types of print, students of all ability levels can build both fluency and comprehension skills. This approach also enables the teacher and students to discuss the relationship between all aspects of literacy—including speaking, listening, thinking, viewing, and reading.

44. C: Mark Twain's book *Adventures of Huckleberry Finn* includes various Southern American dialects to enhance the reader's sense of the setting and characters, so choice C is correct. A dialect encompasses variations from the standard not only in vocabulary but in pronunciation and grammar as well. Choice A is incorrect because *jargon* refers only to vocabulary—specifically to a body of terms used and understood mainly by those in a particular field, profession, or hobby. Choice B is incorrect because the term *slang* also refers to vocabulary that is not considered Standard English but is used by particular age groups or subcultures. Choice D is incorrect because *accent* refers to a set of shifts in pronunciation; the term does not extend to the grammatical and lexical variations that make up a dialect.

45. C: The main role of literature, as described in the passage, is to reflect societal issues and human experiences. The passage discusses how literature serves as a mirror to society, shedding light on issues such as racial injustice and totalitarianism. It emphasizes that literary works like *To Kill a Mockingbird* and *1984* provide valuable insights into the human condition by addressing and reflecting upon these societal issues and human experiences. While literature can certainly entertain and provide glimpses into historical events, the primary focus in this passage is on its role as a reflection of broader societal and human concerns.

46. D: Good children's books should feature plots that are well-constructed and original but not incredible. Narrative books should feature story characters who are believable, which includes their changing (A) and growing as a result of their experiences like real people do, rather than staying the same throughout the story. Adults choosing children's literature should seek books with themes of value to children but avoid books with overtly moralistic themes (B). Likewise, they should avoid books that promote racial, gender, and other stereotypes (C).

47. B: Choice B is correct because dialogue can be used to bring themes and meanings into clearer focus and change the course of the plot. Choice A is incorrect because dialogue can be used to advance the plot and to develop characters. Choice C is incorrect because dialogue should not be used merely to break up exposition, and it does not by itself slow the pace of the story. Choice D is incorrect because dialogue can be used to reproduce real-life speech patterns and to add drama to a story.

48. C: Only the genre of drama includes stage directions, which tell actors where, how, and what they should do physically in plays, which are written to be performed. Plots (A) are found in plays, novels, short stories, and even some poems. Characters (B) are also found in all of these genres. And many plays, particularly early (e.g., ancient Greek; Shakespeare's and other Elizabethan/Renaissance playwrights' work, etc.) as well as some modern and postmodern ones, are written in rhymed and/or free verse (D).

49. A: In both the fictional narrative genre and the nonfictional informational genre, the author will demonstrate some individual writing style; even very factual and objective expositional writing will reveal some personal stylistic characteristics. Labeled diagrams and photos are more likely to be found in informational nonfiction. The majority of books with excitement and drama are fictional narratives (some informational nonfiction books are presented in narrative form and include excitement, especially in children's literature, but these are the minority). Themes and plots are also literary elements associated with fictional narrative.

50. C: The word *literature* has multiple meanings. A general meaning is all the written works in a given language, such as English literature. It can also mean the profession of a writer or author. Literature is also used to mean any kind of printed materials, like a company's promotional or informational literature, including pamphlets, brochures, and the like. However, in research fields, literature typically means all the research previously published on a given subject, such as research on self-correction in the psychology field of applied behavior analysis or on instructional strategies in the English language arts field of writing instruction.

51. B: Mood refers to the emotions evoked in the reader by the literary work, whereas tone refers to the emotions or attitude of the author toward the subject matter or audience, making choice B correct. Choice C is the reverse of this, so it is not correct. Choice A is incorrect because mood and tone do not mean the same thing. Though mood and tone have different meanings, neither one is associated with particular techniques; the same literary techniques could be used for either purpose, so choice D is incorrect.

52. D: In literature and in media, storytellers often use the color red to symbolize a number of concepts: red can signal importance, danger, love, or simply draw the viewer or reader to the particular object in question. The question prompt tells you directly that the red objects signify that the main character is seeing a clue to solving the mystery. In essence, anything colored red represents, or symbolizes, a clue.

53. C: Realist authors strive to represent reality as closely as possible, even in fiction. They avoid exaggeration, which satire often employs to ridicule social behaviors. Though irony is particularly key in satire, realists often use it as well, such as in O. Henry's "The Gift of the Magi," so choice A is not correct. Both genres may involve writing in a serious tone, ruling out choice B. Jonathan Swift intensifies the satirical effects of "A Modest Proposal" by making absurd and even horrific recommendations in an ostensibly serious tone. Finally, choice D is not correct because vernacular dialogue is used in both genres, though generally for different purposes.

54. B: Early ballad themes included jealousy, betrayal, murder, war, famine, poverty, etc. as well as love; early sonnet themes included politics, social standing, satire, etc. as well as love. Both genres have prominently featured expressions of love. The sonnet has five main kinds (A): the Petrarchan/Italian, Occitan, Shakespearean/English, Spenserian, and Modern; the ballad has developed many more variations in form. Originally the ballad was often set to music, and it was later associated with operas and musicals; the sonnet originated in dramatic plays and medieval courts. Though some sonnets have been set to music, the sonnet did not originate with music (C). The standard ballad meter is iambic heptameter, albeit with variations; the standard sonnet meter is iambic pentameter (D).

55. A: One major defining characteristic of the ballad is its narrative function. Traditional ballads tell stories of love, jealousy, revenge, murder, etc.; broadside ballads were composed to entertain and inform the common people about current events; literary ballads enabled intellectuals and the socially elite to express themselves artistically. Historical functions of the sonnet include demonstrating one's skill writing in a highly structured poetic form (b); being featured prominently in theatrical plays (c) (some early plays included ballads, but not to the extent of sonnets); and satirizing romantic, political, and social issues of the time (d).

56. B: Satire is a genre of writing that may be used in informational as well as literary (and informational literary) texts to ridicule human and social faults through various indirect devices, including irony (A), i.e., saying the opposite of what one means; overstatement (C), i.e., exaggerating; and/or understatement (D), i.e., minimizing the importance or seriousness of something in describing it.

57. A: In an essay, the writer defends an opinion by giving reasons for that opinion. Biographies are written to narrate the life of a person. Memoirs detail a person's own life and do not defend opinions. Informational texts are factual.

58. A: Alphabet books, wordless picture books, and easy-to-read books all promote skills important for children beginning to become readers. The other genres are more suitable for older children with well-developed reading skills.

59. D: Children's literature is not meant to instruct students in sciences, such as mathematics and biology; textbooks have that goal. Children's literature is designed to enhance moral values, instruct through entertaining stories, and promote a life-long interest in reading.

60. B: Authors of informational texts may occasionally explicitly state their point of view, but there are more cases where the author is acting as an expert, a neutral observer, or some other ostensibly objective voice. Therefore, readers will often need to infer the author's point of view. Choice A is incorrect because there is no requirement in informational writing that the author's point of view be part of the main idea. Choice C is incorrect because seeing the author's point of view is generally easier when the author is extreme or opinionated and harder when they seem neutral or balanced. This also means that some analysis is usually required, but the need for analysis does not indicate that the writing is poor, so choice D is incorrect.

61. D: Generally speaking, the following story elements take place in sequential order:

Exposition: refers to background information and actions in a story that describe the setting, characters, etc.

Rising action: events in the plot that lead up to the critical event or turning point

Climax: critical event, dramatic scene, or turning point in the story

Falling action: resulting events and actions following the conflict

Resolution: all actions and events are resolved and addressed

Teaching students about the plot elements they can find in most stories will help them develop many skills, including comparisons/contrasts, plot analysis, reading comprehension, etc.

62. A: This choice accurately reflects the author's purpose of introducing the main character, Holden Caulfield, and establishing his perspective on the world. The opening paragraph sets the stage for Holden's disillusionment with society and his struggles with conformity and hypocrisy. Choice B is incorrect because the opening paragraph doesn't establish a lighthearted and optimistic tone. Choice C is incorrect because the opening paragraph doesn't provide a comprehensive summary of the novel's plot. It primarily focuses on Holden's character and his initial thoughts. Choice D is incorrect because the opening paragraph doesn't explicitly attempt to persuade readers to agree with Holden's views. It presents his perspective without necessarily endorsing it.

63. A: The haiku, originating in Japanese poetry and since adopted in English-language poetry, is a short poem of only three lines, often with 17 syllables, with the first and third lines having five syllables and the second line having seven syllables. (In Japanese there are many other rules, which become complicated in comparison to the English version.) Because this syllable pattern is a defining characteristic of English-language haiku, choice A is correct. Haiku are typically unrhymed, so they do not have a rhyme scheme (B). Similarly, they do not employ any regular meter (C). Because haiku are typically 17 syllables or fewer, they do not involve long narratives (D).

64. A: Blogs (short for "web logs") are published online, where anybody with Internet access may read them. Bloggers may post occasionally, monthly, weekly, daily, or whenever they want. It is not uncommon for bloggers to post weekly or daily. Journals are more typical for private entries, similar to diaries. People often make journal entries daily or less often, similarly to blog posts but less publicly. (Some people also publish journals—in print or online as collections in books or e-books, or as ongoing online publications similar to blogs. However, journal writing is more often private, whereas blogging never is.) Letters are typically to others, not private (except for therapeutic letters written to vent emotions but never sent); and though sometimes published online (such as letters to the editor, open letters, or newsletters, among others), usually not daily. Essays are typically not written daily and privately or published online. Speeches are typically written for oral delivery, not daily online publication or as private activities.

65. D: Literary dramatic works, i.e., comedies, tragedies, and other plays, are divided into major sections called acts (A) (even one-act plays have an "act"), and each act is subdivided into scenes (B). Each scene typically is defined by being in a different place and/or time and/or by involving different characters and/or action. Shakespeare and many other playwrights (e.g., ancient Greek, Medieval, Renaissance, Elizabethan, etc.) composed their dramas in poetic verse, so these include stanzas (C), the poetic version of paragraphs. Chapters (D) are divisions not of dramas but of fictional and nonfictional books.

66. A: It is important to evaluate specific reading skills, such as phonemic awareness, in a variety of contexts. Reading aloud with Abi allowed his teacher to notice that he consistently misread words beginning with digraphs. Digraphs are sounds in which two distinct letters, when combined, produce a single third sound (e.g., when *s* and *h* produce the *-sh* sound). Blends are words in which two letters produce a third sound which is a combination of both sounds put together (e.g., *b* and *l* combined to make *b*). The only set of words consisting only of digraphs is choice A.

67. B: Students could recognize the signal words. A is incorrect because defining historical events would not help recognition of comparison and contrast or cause and effect. C is incorrect since a timeline would not help recognition of comparison and contrast or cause and effect. D is incorrect since maps would not help recognition of comparison and contrast or cause and effect.

68. B: Slogans are catchphrases that advertisers want consumers to remember and associate with their brands. They are generally reinforced through repetition. Pathos is a persuasive technique that involves appeals to emotion. A bandwagon appeal advises using a brand because everybody else does (i.e., through popularity/peer pressure). A testimonial is a statement by someone (usually a celebrity or other consumer) endorsing/supporting a brand.

69. C: When students write for their classmates, they should use language that is more informal and age-appropriate, not more sophisticated (A). Jargon also gives the general impression of confusing language where simpler language would be effective. When describing a procedure to a colleague, especially one who is considered an expert, a writer should not need to use simple language (B), as the colleague will likely understand relevant technical or sophisticated language. When writing for younger children, students should use more vivid and entertaining language (C), including some humor when appropriate. When asking parental permission for more independent activities, students should use language that seems more mature and serious rather than using humor (D).

70. B: There are many, many factors that affect reading comprehension in various proportions, depending on the student. Generally speaking, students must be able to recognize vocabulary, decode unfamiliar words, and monitor their own understanding in order to comprehend a given text. In Choice A, all of these factors could affect comprehension; written language development and breakfast, however, are probably less important than the set of factors in Choice B. In Choice C, the factors seem to relate primarily to a student's understanding of the words in the text—vocabulary, sight words, and the ability to look up words. However, students must understand more than simply the words on the page; they must understand the relationships between the words and the underlying meaning of the whole text. In Choice D, classroom participation and performance in other subjects does not necessarily indicate or affect comprehension skills.

71. C: Researchers and educators have found that reading fluency and reading comprehension have a reciprocal relationship: the more fluently a student can read, the more able the student's brain is to process the meaning of text. For example, developing automaticity of word identification enhances comprehension. Conversely, the better a student can understand the text, the more fluently she or he can read it. Therefore, while (A) and (B) are both true, each represents only half of the relationship whereas (C) indicates the relationship's mutual nature. (D) is incorrect as reading fluency and reading comprehension are interrelated components in deriving meaning from text and not separate.

72. B: Jamie's teacher is teaching the class about many aspects of Mexican culture. It can be assumed that Jamie has prior knowledge of this topic, which comes in part from his family's past travels. While Jamie is engaged in the lesson, the verbal instruction and photographs "activate" or inspire recall of his prior knowledge of Spanish vocabulary. Jamie would not likely have been able to access this information without the visual and verbal cues, although it was still stored in his long-term memory.

73. D: Prosody is not an element of metacognition. Metacognition means a reader's awareness of their own reading processes as they improve reading comprehension. Other elements of metacognition include awareness of areas in the text that the reader does not comprehend and an understanding of how the text is structured.

74. B: A KWL chart allows students to list they **K**now about a subject before they read, what they **W**ant to know or learn about it, and what they have **L**earned about it after reading. This is a good example of a research-based instructional strategy for activating students' prior knowledge. The teacher giving the students background information is the opposite of finding out what they already know. The teacher asking students what they know about the subject after they have read a text is also the opposite of the goal. Activating prior knowledge before reading enables students to build upon what they already know when they begin reading, as successful readers do, versus beginning to read without thinking, as less successful readers do. Similarly, the teacher should ask students their opinions and reactions about a topic before they read, not after, to activate their existing knowledge.

75. D: When students ask themselves how the information in a text they are reading fits with what they already know, they are relating the text to their own prior knowledge, which increases their reading comprehension. Students should not only ask themselves what kinds of "expert questions" fit the subject matter of the text (A)—e.g., classification, physical, and chemical properties are typical question topics in science; genre, character, plot, and theme are typical of literature questions; sequence, cause-and-effect, and comparison-contrast questions are typical of history—but also what questions the material brings up for them personally (B). It is necessary and important for students to ask themselves continually how each text portion relates to its chapter's main ideas (C) as they read to optimize their reading comprehension and retention.

76. D: Students typically enjoy watching film versions of literature, especially when the text is challenging to read. An important part of media consumption is building skills to deconstruct the embedded ideas and messages. The teacher in this scenario wants the students to think about how the structure and content of the film affects their understanding of a classic story. In choices A and B, students are assigned to state their opinions about certain aspects of the film or play, but are not asked to critically analyze a specific message. Choice C simply creates a rather tedious assignment that will yield a rote list of examples. Choice D targets the unique setting of the film and encourages students to think about why the film's creators might have chosen to adapt the story in such a way, which is likely to suggest that the content of the story is relevant to people in any era or setting.

77. B: Integrated curriculum is vital to student growth and to fostering a love of learning. In reality, all subject areas are related, and a good teacher will find ways to highlight the connection of concepts across the curriculum. In choice B, the science teacher provides a way to help students study for a test. However, she would probably be better advised to work with the students on comprehension and retention before test time arrives. She could use a variety of previewing and reviewing skills, as well as creative ways to bring the information to life during class discussions and activities. This teacher might also benefit from discussing the situation with a language arts teacher to get ideas on how to build skills in reading for information, main ideas, and supporting concepts.

78. A: The process of actively constructing meaning from reading is interactive, in that it involves the text itself, the person reading it, and the setting in which the reading is done. These three elements influence each other, and this is the concept indicated by the term *interactive* in the question, so choice A is correct. Choice B is a better definition of the *strategic* aspect of the process. Choice C and Choice D are better definitions of the *adaptable* aspect of the process.

79. B: Previewing information is a method by which students can work to improve their own unguided reading comprehension. During the previewing process, students consider the topic at hand, what they already know about it, and what they would like to learn or believe they will learn. Previewing helps students to approach reading for the purpose of comprehension ("reading to learn") and retention. In Choice "a", students will already be familiar with the text if they have already seen the movie; therefore, their previewing will be affected by familiarity with the text. The same is true for Choice "c", as the students have already read the novel. In Choice "d", previewing the poetry will indeed increase familiarity with the poems. However, reading poetry is typically not a process that involves "reading to learn." Instead, poetry is more often approached as a pleasure-reading activity or an opportunity for literary analysis. Allowing students to preview science material helps them actively learn to read for information and will aid them in other subjects.

80. C: There is currently a wide variety of technology resources available that can support class instruction. However, teachers must choose carefully in order to ensure that the technology is useful and relevant to the intended learning outcomes for the class. The language lab described allows students to experience text through both listening and reading, thereby utilizing different processes in the brain. The interactive modules also support decoding and comprehension skills that go along with the texts. This use of technology reinforces important skills in a way that will be unique and interesting for the students.

81. C: The most helpful strategy for discerning which of two homonyms (sound-alike words) is correct without knowing the spelling is its surrounding context of the sentence, paragraph, and/or book and subject matter. For example, "Mexico cedes land" and "Mexico seeds land" sound the same, but if the context continues "to the United States," the meaning of "cedes" applies. Pictures (A) help children identify unknown words rather than differentiate homonyms. Phonics (B) help students sound out unfamiliar words, not differentiate meanings. Grammar (D) can help when one homonym is a verb and the other a noun, for example; but "cedes" and "seeds" are the same part of speech with different meanings, so grammar alone does not help as much as context.

82. A: Expository texts are nonfiction works that give information, like how-to instructions or facts about a given subject. Therefore the most appropriate inferences for the reader to draw would be about cause-and-effect relationships, such as in history books, and/or about problems and their solutions. Reader inferences about what events occurred and things people did are more appropriate when reading a nonfictional biography or autobiography. Reader inferences about what the author wants the audience to believe and about ideas that support the author's message are more appropriate when reading persuasive or argumentative text, wherein the author works to convince readers of a position, opinion, or argument.

83. A: Experts do advise communications presenters to combine two or three types of media for the most effectiveness, rather than limiting themselves to only one (B). The presenter's budget will also necessarily influence their choice of media (C). For example, TV is more expensive than radio; radio is more expensive than paying a PR writer for print communications; and some presenters can produce their own news releases and photos at no additional cost. How long a communication is will affect the media choice (D), e.g., in terms of costs and of maintaining audience attention.

84. A: A slide show presentation is designed as a visual aid to summarize and highlight the main points in a speaker's talk. Slide show presentation slides commonly feature brief verbal phrases and sentences; are often numbered or bulleted; and also may include pictures, diagrams, graphs, and more. The slides not only visualize the speaker's main points for audiences, guide listeners through the presentation, and facilitate note-taking and outlining by listeners, they also help keep the speaker organized and on the subject. The slides provide an outline of the presentation; the speaker supplies the additional details. A poster is a visual aid, but not a technological tool. It would also not add as much to the presentation as a slide show. A blog and a wiki are both designed for audiences to read online, not to read while someone is speaking or to listen to someone reading them aloud.

85. B: Typical speech is roughly 125 words per minute, while typical thinking is estimated at roughly 500 words per minute. This natural disparity does not make listening less effective than reading. While the slower rate of speech and the faster rate of thought does allow students' minds to wander, teachers can have students make use of this time by instructing them to summarize mentally the speech they hear as an active listening technique. This enables students to process, consider, and manipulate heard information and make richer, more creative decisions about it. Listening and learning share the common characteristics of being both social and reciprocal.

86. D: Choice "a" would be appropriate for class work or homework, but is less likely than other choices to provide a deep understanding of the relationships between oral and spoken word. Choice "b" would address multicultural interest, but would not require interpretation since only recitation is assigned. Choice "c" could allow students to learn more about their classmates' backgrounds, but would require more specific parameters to ensure that both the multicultural and oral learning outcomes were achieved. Choice "c" also does not address the assumption that the classmates' family backgrounds are diverse, which may not be the case. Choice "d" requires students to use their research skills to learn more about another culture. By assigning a first-person narrative, Mr. Callas encourages the students to imagine life from the perspective of another person. This assignment also requires the student to make the transition from research to written assignment to spoken word.

87. A: If you read the question prompt carefully, you will notice that the question refers specifically to language skills. While Choice "c" is important and would likely result from the exercise, it does not signify a specific language skill. Students' motor skills are not likely to significantly improve over the course of one day, eliminating Choice "b". In Choice "d", the assumption that other individuals in the community would be able to interpret sign language is incorrect. But the seminar would indeed provide an opportunity for students to learn about how visual representations affect meaning. Using sign language allows them to hone listening and expression skills simultaneously, as well as to learn how to decode nonverbal expressions.

88. D: Teachers should give students learning English as a second language (ESL) and English language learners (ELLs) clear models and examples of what they expect them to do, how to do it, and how the completed results should look. Stating directions verbally in English alone is insufficient for students learning a foreign language. Teachers must also give ELLs more time to respond because it takes them longer to process the English they hear, mentally translate it into their own language, mentally formulate a response in their own language, translate that mentally into English, and judge whether their translation makes sense before they answer. It typically takes ESLs years before they can "think in English." When using idioms and figures of speech, teachers should explain these to ELLs and add pantomime demonstrations to help them understand. These expressions are not logical and often have no L1 equivalents for ESLs, so they require explicit instruction.

89. D: Teachers can best employ strategic demands on children who are learning new vocabulary by beginning at a low level of demand and moving to high-demand questions. This effectively scaffolds new instruction by building up from simple and easy to complex and difficult. Alternation can be helpful as well, but instructing at a high level early on may result in confusion and frustration, rather than an improved grasp of a concept. (B) describes a constructivist approach to vocabulary, which can work for more abstract concepts. As students naturally encounter a concept, they build their own understanding of how something works. This approach may not be the best method for vocabulary acquisition, as students may arrive at inaccurate meanings. Similarly, (C) suggests keeping the rigor low until students have mastery over the new vocabulary, but vocabulary requires understanding terms in shallow and in deep ways and requires interaction with the word in a variety of applications to truly master a concept. Oversimplification can lead to inaccurate knowledge and possibly even frustration. Instead, a teacher should begin with a clear and simple definition and work toward complex applications as students are capable.

90. C: Students will not typically arrive in the classroom with excellent listening skills; these skills must be introduced and honed as any others would be. Students often benefit from previewing material or pointing out what they should be listening *for*, since it will be virtually impossible for them to retain every piece of information proffered during class time. If the information is previewed, they are predisposed to listen carefully to important topics. When asked questions about the information, the teacher will be able to monitor how well they listened, as well as whether they understood what they heard. Choice A does involve listening skills but does not provide direct instruction or a method of monitoring improvement; choices B and D monitor improvement but do not build skills.

91. A: The pragmatic component of oral language development involves learning the rules for using speech that is appropriate to various social situations, including how to speak and when to speak or not speak. The phonological component (B) of oral language development involves learning the rules for putting speech sounds or phonemes into words. The semantic component (C) of oral language development involves learning word meanings and acquiring vocabulary. The syntactic component (D) of oral language development involves learning the rules for combining words in the correct sequence or order to create understandable sentences.

92. C: Each answer can be an effective tool in teaching students to build oral language skills. The question makes clear that the objective is to help students evaluate their own oral language skills, which will assist them in both spoken and written assignments. The only answer choice that involves the students evaluating their own message is choice C. When the students prepare a review/quiz based upon important information, they will be more able to speak specifically to that information. When classmates complete the review, each student can identify any patterns in the questions' answers that give clues as to how well those main ideas were communicated. In this way, the student can evaluate how effective the oral presentation was, without relying on classmates or the teacher.

93. D: A speech differs from an essay in that it is spoken or read aloud to a live audience, where as an essay is published. Because speeches are given at live events, certain components may need to be included that would not be necessary or appropriate in an essay. These components include greetings (to the audience and possibly to honored guests) and thanks (perhaps to the audience for listening or perhaps to those who have helped or influenced the speaker). Therefore, choice D is correct. Choice A is incorrect because speech introductions differ from essay introductions in that they may include some of the elements above. Choice B is incorrect because the body of a speech and the body of an essay should elaborate and provide supporting evidence in a similar fashion. Choice C is incorrect because speech conclusions, while they sometimes need to include information that essay conclusions do not, must be appropriately forceful and engaging, just as essay conclusions should be.

94. D: Teachers should try to avoid shallow notions of what it means to provide cultural or multi-cultural education; in Choice "a", we cannot presume to understand another person by listening to his favorite music or watching a favorite movie. In Choice "b", there is also the assumption that there is a variety of musical tastes in the class, which may not be the case. In fact, if many students pick the same song, it is possible to use that choice to open up dialogue about what they lyrics mean and why they are so popular with the class. Choice "c" is posed in direct opposition to Choice "d". However, Choice "d" suggests what most teachers know to be true: literacy skills are not just important for schoolwork and class work; students must be able to take meaning from a variety of different sources in order to grow into educated adults. Music is an important medium through which students can express themselves and learn about the world around them through comprehension and listening skills.

95. C: Teachers must establish and communicate clear ground rules for students before initiating collaborative classroom discussions. One rule is to prohibit cross talk, which is counterproductive to equitable conversations. Another rule for teachers to set is that students should not interrupt other students when they are speaking (A). An additional good rule is to caution talkative students not to monopolize the conversation (B). Teachers should not only set a ground rule against verbal abuse of classmates, they should additionally set a rule against physical abuse (e.g., shoving, hitting, kicking, biting, etc.), which is not unlikely (D) with younger students and students with behavioral issues.

96. B: English language learners (ELLs) generally benefit from contextual learning of vocabulary because it helps to solidify the meaning and usage of the newly-learned words. Both vocabulary in isolation (a) and vocabulary in volume (b) typically refer to rote memorization, which does not provide the retention benefits or provide the student with contextual experience. Answer (d) is wrong because speech proficiency levels do not necessarily correspond to a student's reading and vocabulary skills.

97. C: An effective teacher technique for meeting learning goals in classroom discussions if students get off the subject is to restate the topics and questions they previously stated. Another good redirection technique is to ask new questions about the same topics. To encourage creative and varied student responses, teachers should ask questions instead of making comments, not vice versa. Teachers making comments discourages students from doing the same, whereas asking questions invites them to offer different feedback. When some students dominate the discussion, a technique whereby teachers can engage more reticent students is to ask less challenging questions, not more: less challenging questions can be answered by any student, even unprepared ones. A checklist based on the class attendance roll is a good way to assess whether all students are participating.

98. D: Asking children to write a list provides them with a visual model that is a side-by-side comparison of the two countries. In creating that visual model, each student first has to organize his or her thoughts mentally, deciding whether each particular item under consideration is shared between both countries or is a difference between them.

99. B: In the Spanish language, the letter h is typically silent. Because the student is an ELL and the USA has many people—both immigrants and those born here—whose first and/or only language is Spanish, this is the first factor to consider among the choices. An articulation disorder (A) is possible, but the teacher should not assume this first with an ELL student. (An SLP evaluation can determine the difference.) While a hearing assessment (C) is always a good idea, if /h/ omission were due to hearing loss the student would likely omit or distort other unvoiced fricatives like /f/, /s/, /ʃ/, and /θ/. If the student had a breathing problem (D), other symptoms would occur in addition to not articulating /h/.

100. D: The concept in question is known as language transfer, also known as L1 interference, in which language features from the first language affects the acquisition of a second language. This is particularly noteworthy in language features that exist in one language, but not in the other. For instance, in English, plural nouns are usually marked by adding *-s* to the end of the word, whereas Chinese does not make use of a plural indicator. This grammatical feature, therefore, is commonly difficult to accurately acquire. Regarding the options in the question, the Chinese written language is ideographic rather than alphabetic (A)—that is, its written symbols represent concepts visually rather than being letters representing speech sounds. Also, the fact that Spanish is much more phonetically regular than English (B) (i.e., many more words are pronounced the same way as they are spelled than in English) contributes different effects to ELL students' English-language literacy development. Therefore, choice C is incorrect.

Practice Test #2

Refer to the following for questions 1–5:

A teacher has an immense set of responsibilities to juggle, but also has access to a number of resources. Multiple people and organizations are available to aid teachers in their work or to augment the educational experiences of the students. One of these resources is the Library Media Center (LMC), which serves both to provide a broader education for students and to share the teaching tasks of the teacher.

The Library Media Center serves to educate students on multiple topics: research, technology, information literacy, and many others. Students are able to obtain hands-on experience in discovering information and learning how to find what they need. The librarian and other library staff guide the students during their time in the LMC, giving the teacher time to focus on other needs such as planning.

The instruction given in the LMC not only offers an extra learning opportunity for students, but also provides extra help in the classroom for teachers. Teachers can use the resources and instruction that the LMC offers to enrich their lessons, link various subjects together, and engage students more deeply in learning. The school library is more than merely a place to read books; it sparks learning.

1. Where in this passage is the main idea stated?

a. The first sentence
b. The second sentence
c. The third sentence
d. The entire first paragraph

2. Which of these choices is the best example of a topic sentence in this passage?

a. The first sentence in the first paragraph
b. The second sentence in the first paragraph
c. The first sentence in the second paragraph
d. The second sentence in the second paragraph

3. Which of the following is a synonym for the word "juggle" in the first sentence?

a. Succeed
b. Balance
c. Waver
d. Toss

4. What is the meaning of the word "augment" in the second sentence?

a. Increase
b. Correct
c. Change
d. Color

5. Which of the following most accurately restates the main idea of the passage?

a. Teachers cannot carry the teaching burden alone, so library staff help them.
b. There are many resources available for teachers if they know where to look.
c. Libraries serve to educate students in many ways and to provide assistance to teachers.
d. A library is more than just a place to find books.

Refer to the following for questions 6–10:

Classroom Management

While each teacher has a unique method of classroom management and cannot be completely categorized as one certain type, most tend toward one of four main styles. These styles depend on the amount of control and involvement a teacher takes. A teacher with both high involvement and high control is Authoritative. An Authoritarian teacher also exhibits a high level of control, but low involvement. Some teachers exhibit high involvement but low control. These teachers are termed Indulgent. Finally, a Permissive teacher has low involvement and low control. The style a teacher uses determines, to a significant degree, both the environment of the classroom and the success of the teaching.

An Authoritative teacher provides a stable environment with clear expectations. Rules are enforced and the teacher is invested in the students, who learn to be responsible and to take on leadership. Students under Authoritarian teachers, on the other hand, can feel uncared for, as behavior is strictly enforced but the teacher may not take time to explain rules and concepts or truly invest in the individuals. Indulgent teachers take time to talk to students and help them but rules are feebly enforced. Students know their teacher cares for them, but this style can lead to a chaotic environment that hampers learning. Permissive teachers allow excess freedom for students and give little direction, which can result in poor behavior and lack of learning.

While each style can have benefits, the Authoritative style is typically the most effective for student learning because it provides an orderly and caring atmosphere. Students know they must behave but they also know the teacher cares about them and will take time to explain concepts and listen to questions. The strictness is tempered by kindness, and students not only learn better but also grow better emotionally in an Authoritative environment.

6. Which of the following is the most accurate meaning of *feebly*, as used in the fourth sentence of paragraph 2?

a. Weakly
b. In a senile fashion
c. Haphazardly
d. Rarely

7. The word *tempered* in the last sentence is closest in meaning to which related word?

a. The noun *temper*, meaning the heat of anger
b. The adjective *temperate*, meaning moderate
c. The noun *temper*, meaning one's disposition
d. The adjective *temperamental*, meaning sensitive

8. Of these choices, where is the main idea of this article best expressed?

a. In the article's title
b. In the first sentence of the first paragraph
c. In the last sentence of the first paragraph
d. In the last sentence of the last paragraph

9. What can be stated about the topic sentences in this selection?

a. The first sentence of each paragraph is that paragraph's topic sentence.
b. None of the three paragraphs has a true topic sentence, only a main idea.
c. The first and third paragraphs begin with a topic sentence, while the second paragraph has no clear topic sentence.
d. Each paragraph concludes with the topic sentence.

10. What best describes the sequence of the paragraphs in this article?

a. Main Idea, Supporting Details, Summary
b. Problem, Solution, Summary
c. Introduction, Cause, Effect
d. Introduction, Supporting Details, Application

Refer to the following for questions 11–13:

But all this—the mysterious, far-reaching hair-line trail, the absence of sun from the sky, the tremendous cold, and the strangeness and weirdness of it all—made no impression on the man. It was not because he was long used to it. He was a newcomer in the land, a chechaquo, and this was his first winter. The trouble with him was that he was without imagination. He was quick and alert in the things of life, but only in the things, and not in the significances. Fifty degrees below zero meant eighty-odd degrees of frost. Such fact impressed him as being cold and uncomfortable, and that was all. It did not lead him to meditate upon his frailty as a creature of temperature, and upon man's frailty in general, able only to live within certain narrow limits of heat and cold; and from there on it did not lead him to the conjectural field of immortality and man's place in the universe. Fifty degrees below zero stood for a bite of frost that hurt and that must be guarded against by the use of mittens, ear-flaps, warm moccasins, and thick socks. Fifty degrees below zero was to him just precisely fifty degrees below zero. That there should be anything more to it than that was a thought that never entered his head.

. . . .

At the man's heels trotted a dog, a big native husky, the proper wolf-dog, gray-coated and without any visible or temperamental difference from its brother, the wild wolf. The animal was depressed by the tremendous cold. It knew that it was no time for travelling. Its instinct told it a truer tale than was told to the man by the man's judgment. In reality, it was not merely colder than fifty below zero; it was colder than sixty below, than seventy below. It was seventy-five below zero. Since the freezing-point is thirty-two above zero, it meant that one hundred and seven degrees of frost obtained. The dog did not know anything about thermometers. Possibly in its brain there was no sharp consciousness of a condition of very cold such as was in the man's brain. But the brute had its instinct. It experienced a vague but menacing apprehension that subdued it and made it slink along at the man's heels, and that made it question eagerly every unwonted movement of the man as if expecting him to go into camp or to seek shelter somewhere and build a fire. The dog had learned fire, and it wanted fire, or else to burrow under the snow and cuddle its warmth away from the air.

[Adapted from Jack London, "To Build a Fire" (1902)]

11. In this short story, the main character struggles against the cold and eventually freezes to death. Given this information, which of the following devices is the author using in the first paragraph of this passage?

a. First-person point of view
b. Hyperbole
c. Onomatopoeia
d. Foreshadowing

12. What is the point of view used in this passage?

a. First person
b. First person plural
c. Third person limited
d. Third person omniscient

13. Which statement best captures the author's meaning in the statement, "The trouble with him was that he was without imagination"?

I. The man was not smart.
II. The man did not need imagination because he was rational.
III. The man did not have the foresight to realize that he was putting himself in danger.

a. I only
b. II only
c. III only
d. I and II

Refer to the following for questions 14–17:

It is a truth universally acknowledged, that a single man in possession of a good fortune, must be in want of a wife.

However little known the feelings or views of such a man may be on his first entering a neighbourhood, this truth is so well fixed in the minds of the surrounding families, that he is considered the rightful property of some one or other of their daughters.

"My dear Mr. Bennet," said his lady to him one day, "have you heard that Netherfield Park is let at last?"

Mr. Bennet replied that he had not.

"But it is," returned she; "for Mrs. Long has just been here, and she told me all about it."

Mr. Bennet made no answer.

"Do you not want to know who has taken it?" cried his wife impatiently.

"You want to tell me, and I have no objection to hearing it."

This was invitation enough.

"Why, my dear, you must know, Mrs. Long says that Netherfield is taken by a young man of large fortune from the north of England; that he came down on Monday in a chaise and four to see the place, and was so much delighted with it, that he agreed with Mr. Morris immediately; that he is to take possession before Michaelmas, and some of his servants are to be in the house by the end of next week."

"What is his name?"

"Bingley."

"Is he married or single?"

"Oh! Single, my dear, to be sure! A single man of large fortune; four or five thousand a year. What a fine thing for our girls!"

"How so? How can it affect them?"

"My dear Mr. Bennet," replied his wife, "how can you be so tiresome! You must know that I am thinking of his marrying one of them."

"Is that his design in settling here?"

"Design! Nonsense, how can you talk so! But it is very likely that he may fall in love with one of them, and therefore you must visit him as soon as he comes."

"I see no occasion for that. You and the girls may go, or you may send them by themselves, which perhaps will be still better, for as you are as handsome as any of them, Mr. Bingley may like you the best of the party."

[Adapted from Jane Austen, *Pride and Prejudice* (1813)]

14. What is the central idea of this selection?

a. A new neighbor is due to arrive who may become good friends with Mr. and Mrs. Bennet.
b. A new neighbor is due to arrive who may be a prospective husband for one of the Bennet daughters.
c. A new neighbor is due to arrive who may be a good business connection for Mr. Bennet.
d. A new neighbor is due to arrive who has already expressed an interest in marrying one of the Bennet daughters.

15. Which of the following statements best describes Mrs. Bennet's feelings about her husband as indicated by this selection?

a. Mrs. Bennet is tired of her husband.
b. Mrs. Bennet is exasperated by her husband.
c. Mrs. Bennet is afraid of her husband.
d. Mrs. Bennet is indifferent toward her husband.

16. This selection is set in England at the beginning of the 19th century. Drawing on information from this selection, what could you conclude was a primary goal for young women in England during this time period?

a. To marry a man who wants a wife
b. To marry a man with money
c. To entertain the neighbors
d. To find and attract wealthy neighbors to move nearby

17. "Is that his design in settling here?"

What does the word design mean in the context of this selection?

a. Intention
b. Drawing
c. Creation
d. Improvisation

Refer to the following for questions 18–22:

There Will Come Soft Rains

By Sara Teasdale

There will come soft rains and the smell of the ground,
And swallows circling with their shimmering sound;

And frogs in the pools singing at night,
And wild plum trees in tremulous white;

Robins will wear their feathery fire
Whistling their whims on a low fence-wire;

And not one will know of the war, not one
Will care at last when it is done.

Not one would mind, neither bird nor tree
If mankind perished utterly;

And Spring herself, when she woke at dawn,
Would scarcely know that we were gone.

18. How many stanzas does this poem have?

a. 2
b. 4
c. 6
d. 12

19. Which line is the best example of personification used in the poem?

a. "And frogs in the pools singing at night"
b. "Robins will wear their feathery fire"
c. "And not one will know of the war, not one"
d. "And Spring herself, when she woke at dawn"

20. The *we* used in the final line ("Would scarcely know that we were gone") refers to:

a. All of mankind
b. The victors of the war
c. Americans
d. The poet and the reader

21. This poem is an example of a(n)

a. sonnet.
b. rhymed verse.
c. free verse.
d. lyric.

22. Which of these statements offers the best summary of the poem?

a. Nature does not care about the affairs of mankind.
b. It is the government's responsibility to fight a war.
c. War has a devastating impact on nature.
d. Wars should not be fought in the spring.

Refer to the following for questions 23–25:

The Nigerian Letter Fraud

Nigerian letter frauds are variations of advance fee schemes in which a letter, mailed from Nigeria, offers the recipient the "opportunity" to share in millions of dollars that the author, a self-proclaimed government official, is trying to transfer illegally out of Nigeria. The victim receives a letter or email asking him to send personal information: blank letterhead stationery, bank name and account numbers and other identifying information. Eventually, the scheme attempts to get the willing victim, who has demonstrated a propensity for larceny by responding to the invitation, to send money to the author of the letter in Nigeria in several installments of increasing amounts for a variety of reasons. Payment of taxes, bribes to government officials, and legal fees are often described in great detail with the promise that all expenses will be reimbursed as soon as the funds are spirited out of Nigeria. In reality, the millions of dollars do not exist and the victim gets nothing. In fact, once the victim stops sending money, the perpetrators have been known to use the personal information that they received to impersonate the victim, draining bank accounts and credit card balances. While such an invitation strikes most of us as a laughable hoax, millions of dollars in losses are caused by these schemes annually.

23. This paragraph is best described as which of the following?

a. Factual reporting
b. Humor
c. Fiction
d. Poetry

24. What is a "propensity for larceny?"

a. A desire for compensation
b. A proclivity for theft
c. A talent for robbery
d. A disinclination for pilferage

25. What does the author conclude about the Nigerian letter gambit?

a. It is a laughable attempt to defraud people that has little chance of success.
b. It is a good reason not to open email attachments.
c. It is sometimes legitimate.
d. It is surprisingly successful.

26. When an author uses rhetoric to support his or her point of view or purpose in an informational text, by which of these means can they best provide supporting evidence?

a. Relating personal anecdotes
b. Making analogies to clarify ideas
c. Describing relevant case studies
d. Laying out premises and conclusions

27. When writing an essay, which of the following tasks is best to complete first?

a. List all details supporting each main point
b. Decide how to sequence main points
c. Organize details in a logical order
d. Narrow possible topics down to one main idea

28. Among seven steps a reader can take to evaluate an author's argument in persuasive writing, which of the first four steps should the reader take *first*?

a. Evaluate the author's objectivity regarding the issue.
b. Judge how relevant the supporting evidence provided is.
c. Identify the author's assumptions regarding the issue.
d. Identify what supporting evidence the author offers.

29. Which of the following is a primary function of argumentative writing?

a. To explain a process to readers
b. To articulate a concept for readers
c. To present new information to readers
d. To prove a point that will convince readers

30. Among these procedural devices that help students plan and revise writing, which is helpful as an aid for remembering key sets of information?

a. Outlines
b. Checklists
c. Mnemonic devices
d. Graphic organizers

31. Which of the following statements is true about outlines?

a. They allow the writer to visualize the relationships between supporting details.
b. They help students learn to write but are not often used by experienced writers.
c. They allow writers to plan the sequence of their supporting details.
d. They require that writers come up with several sentences to summarize each point.

32. Among effective research practices, which of the following is most accurate?

a. If one finds unlimited material, one should broaden one's research question.
b. If one finds too little related material, one's research question is too narrow.
c. If one knows the research question first, one can get lost among all the data.
d. If one finds no existing literature on a new topic, no type of searching helps.

33. If a teacher assigns students to pairs for cooperative writing partnerships, which of the following should their activities include?

a. One student should write, and the other should review the work.
b. Each partner in a pair takes turns being the writer and the reviewer.
c. Each student should provide only positive feedback to the other.
d. Each student should give only constructive feedback to the other.

34. Which of the following approaches to writing instruction is characterized by setting clear writing goals, observing concrete data, and applying learning to written composition?

a. Prewriting strategies
b. Modeling strategies
c. Inquiry strategies
d. Process writing

35. What do research studies find about student collaboration relative to effective writing instruction?

a. Cooperative learning does not apply to teaching writing.
b. Cooperative learning is an effective practice for writing.
c. Cooperative learning needs no structure from teachers.
d. Cooperative learning needs structure, not expectations.

36. When using research-based writing instruction strategies, which should be gradually faded?

a. Brainstorming
b. Explicit instruction
c. Teacher modeling
d. Collaborative work

37. Which of the following statements is most accurate about writing the introduction of an essay?

a. The introduction should move from the broad and general to the focused and specific.
b. The introduction should save the most attention-getting material for later in the work.
c. The introduction should move from the focused and specific to the broad and general.
d. The introduction should use the technique of starting essays with dictionary definitions.

38. Regarding the standard conventions for written English when evaluating student writing, which of the following reflects the function of writing rather than its form?

a. The length of the student's composition
b. Appropriate content in the composition
c. Word usage in a student's composition
d. The spelling in a student's composition

39. Which of the following is true?

a. a simile compares different things by using a word such as like or as.
b. a metaphor compares different things by using a word such as like or as.
c. a metaphor makes a comparison while a simile does not.
d. a simile makes a comparison while a metaphor does not.

40. An understanding of the meanings of prefixes and suffixes such as *dis, mis, un, re, able,* and *ment* is important primarily for:

a. Reading comprehension
b. Word recognition
c. Vocabulary building
d. Reading fluency

41. Which of the following is an example of a case when second-person narrative voice or point of view might be more effective than first- or third- person?

a. An informative text explaining how to install a piece of equipment correctly
b. A fictional text recounting a dream the narrator had the night before
c. A persuasive essay concerning a political viewpoint
d. A petition written by a group of people desiring change

42. Which of these is most accurate regarding persuasive techniques used in advertising?

a. Repetition and appeals to audience sentiment are both effective persuasive tools.
b. Qualifiers, better known as "weasel words," typically accompany understated claims.
c. Persuasion via humor is used more often in news and advocacy than in advertising.
d. Hyperbole, superlatives, and intensifiers are considered hallmarks of cheap advertising.

43. Which mode of writing is most suitable for the purpose of encouraging the reading audience to explore ideas and consider various potential associated responses?

a. Narrative
b. Expository
c. Persuasive
d. Speculative

44. *Beowulf* is an epic poem that is important because it is often viewed as the first significant work of English literature. Although it was first written in AD 700, it is thought to be even hundreds of years older than that. It is believed that the story of *Beowulf* was told for centuries before it ever made its way on to paper. It is still taught today in various schools and universities.

***Beowulf* is a significant poem because:**

a. It was first written down in AD 700.
b. It was told for centuries before it was written down.
c. It is still taught today in academic settings.
d. It is the first important work of English literature.

45. In explanatory writing, which of the following does the writer typically NOT do?

a. Differentiate among the members of a given category
b. Assume some information is factual, accurate, or true
c. Prove certain information is factual, accurate and true
d. Define terms, analyze processes, or develop concepts

46. In character development analysis, which of the following is NOT likely to be helpful?

a. Paying attention to observations the narrator makes about a character
b. Observing apparent contradictions in a character's thoughts and behavior
c. Determining how a character could be used differently by the author
d. Noting how the narrator and the other characters speak differently about a character

47. A teacher assigns a project in which students must compare excerpts from the Charles Dickens novel they are reading in class and an article from the week's newspaper. The teacher has chosen a specific passage from the novel. The students can choose the newspaper excerpts, as long as they are of similar lengths. The students must then write a short essay comparing the two. What is this teacher hoping to show her students?

a. That Dickens' writing style is journalistic and that he informed much of what is considered to be current journalistic philosophy.
b. That there are links between the students' lives and what they read in class; the relationships are there if they make an effort to see them.
c. That you can compare even two unlike things.
d. That there are distinct differences between the way meaning is constructed in daily life and in literature; different processes must be applied.

48. Which finding, if true, would most directly support the student's claim?

In a recent class discussion, a student passionately argued that literature has a profound impact on society and individuals. The student claimed that literature not only reflects societal values and challenges but also actively shapes our perceptions, beliefs, and behaviors. To support this assertion, the student highlighted the power of literature to evoke empathy, provide diverse perspectives, and spark critical thinking. The student contended that literature serves as a mirror in which we see ourselves and as a window through which we explore the world. However, some of the student's peers questioned this perspective, suggesting that literature may have a limited influence in the modern digital age. To resolve the debate, the class decided to investigate whether there is empirical evidence linking literature to societal attitudes and behaviors.

a. Modern society places a greater emphasis on visual media, making literature less influential in shaping public opinion.
b. Studies have shown that individuals who read literature featuring diverse characters and experiences exhibit increased empathy and tolerance in their attitudes.
c. Literary classics from different time periods consistently receive lower readership and engagement compared to contemporary literature.
d. There is no substantial correlation between the type of literature individuals read and their beliefs or actions.

49. Which genre of children's literature is most likely to begin "Once upon a time..." and conclude with a happy ending?

a. Modern fantasy
b. Picture books
c. Traditional
d. Poetry books

50. Among genres of literature, which is typically the most condensed or verbally economical?

a. A play
b. A novel
c. A poem
d. An essay

51. Which author was among the founders of the Modernist movement and authored *A Room of One's Own* in 1929?

a. Fyodor Dostoevsky
b. Francis Bacon
c. Charles Dickens
d. Virginia Woolf

52. One element of literature establishes the emotional climate in a work through the author's choice of setting, details, imagery, objects, and words. One example of this element is mystery. Which of the following is this element?

a. Tone
b. Mood
c. Conflict
d. Point of view

53. In which genre does the literature rely on the reader's suspension of disbelief about magical and mythical creatures?

a. Science fiction
b. Fantasy
c. Action and adventure
d. Historical fiction

54. What is the general purpose of the *roman à clef* form in novels and other literature?

a. To give readers a greater challenge in understanding
b. To disguise truths too threatening to state explicitly
c. To confuse readers deliberately by hiding meanings
d. To distance readers from traumatic experiences

55. What most accurately identifies the kind(s) of opportunities teachers are expected to give students with respect to literature?

a. To read different literary genres independently only
b. To hear literature read aloud in addition to reading it
c. To respond to literature by writing and speaking on it
d. To read, listen, and respond to literature and to interact with other students

56. Among these literary genres, in which pair has one *most* been used within the other?

a. Nonfiction prose within poetry
b. Fictional prose within drama
c. Poetry within fictional drama
d. Poetry within nonfiction prose

57. What is a primary distinction between the fiction subgenres of historical fiction and science fiction?

a. One is set in the real past; the other is set in the possible future.
b. One is based on facts; the other is based on speculations.
c. One is concerned with events; the other is concerned with inventions.
d. Answers (A) and (B) both apply; (C) is not necessarily true.

58. Which of the following characteristics can the fiction subgenres of historical fiction and science fiction be said to share in common?

a. Both are always about fictional characters.
b. Both are always about imaginary events.
c. Both are always speculative in some way.
d. Both are always closely aligned with facts.

59. In the genre of poetry, which of the following is the term for a group of related ideas that is expressed in multiple lines of text and separated from other such groups by spaces?

a. Verse
b. Stanza
c. Refrain
d. Paragraph

60. Consider a paired reading exercise that aims to help students understand an informational text. Which of the following will be a necessary part of the exercise?

a. Identifying genres that the work fits into
b. Identifying the main idea and supporting details
c. Identifying prior knowledge that both students have
d. Identifying any external texts that support the author's view

61. In selecting literature for children, the most important first step a teacher should perform is to evaluate

a. Whether the characters are interesting
b. Whether the plots are appealing
c. Class composition and preferences
d. The reading level of the material

62. Good books for a second-grader who is interested in reading fantasy fiction include:

a. *The BFG* and *Charlie and the Chocolate Factory*
b. *Harry Potter and the Sorcerer's Stone* and *The Golden Compass*
c. *Nate the Great* and *Amelia Bedelia*
d. *Commander Toad in Space* and *The Mouse and the Motorcycle*

63. What is the term for the final resolution of a fictional plot?

a. Exposition
b. Rising action
c. Falling action
d. Denouement

64. To improve student reading comprehension of a text passage that is entirely descriptive with no plot, which of the following strategies can a teacher provide that would help most?

a. Identifying the sensory details
b. Retelling the passage contents
c. Previewing the passage of text
d. Self-monitoring during reading

65. Which choice describes an appropriate alternative to round robin reading?

a. All students read together, simultaneously speaking the text aloud.
b. Students break into pairs assigned by the teacher to take turns reading the text while the teacher circulates among the pairs to guide and assess the students.
c. The teacher reads aloud to the students before engaging in a class discussion about what they have learned.
d. Students work on independent assignments while the teacher listens to students read individually.

66. After the eleventh-grade students read the World War II story of the brave German theologian Dietrich Bonhoeffer, a Lutheran minister who defied Hitler, the teacher had students explain their personal definitions of faith. This activity is likely to benefit students PRIMARILY by

a. introducing them to World War II.
b. teaching them about Germany.
c. involving them in the concept of faith.
d. providing a multicultural true story.

67. Of the following criteria for critically evaluating how effective an informational text author's methods of appealing to the reading audience are, which is related to whether readers believed the author, and why they did or did not?

a. Clarity
b. Accuracy
c. Cohesion
d. Credibility

68. A class reads an essay about the benefits to youth of pet ownership. The author's position is very clear: she believes young people should be given the responsibility of taking care of pets. The author cites facts, research studies, and statistics to strengthen her position. This type of writing is called:

a. Expository
b. Narrative
c. Persuasive
d. Didactic

Refer to the following for question 69:

Valeria is a bright sixth-grader who struggles with reading fluency. She comes from a predominantly Spanish-speaking home and has only lived in the United States for two years. Her teacher plans to use the guided oral reading strategy to help increase Valeria's reading skills. She also plans to use Valeria's scheduled media time to help work on her fluency.

69. Which of the following computer activities/games would be most beneficial to use during Valeria's media time?

a. Valeria can select from a variety of high-interest texts and read aloud what she sees on the screen.
b. Valeria can hear high-frequency sight and vocabulary words in her headphones and get points for "zapping" (clicking) the correct matching word on her screen.
c. Valeria can practice typing in a keyboarding program to build her speed and accuracy in writing reports and papers.
d. Valeria can surf a limited and pre-approved number of internet sites to read on subjects of her choosing.

70. Mrs. Taylor is working with a diverse group of fifth-graders. She introduces a lesson and project that students can work on once they have finished their regular class work. Students may visit a section of the classroom where they can listen to a lesson via headphones on ancient Egyptian hieroglyphics and look at various library books on the subject. Students are then expected to create their own hieroglyphics that they can use to tell a short story. Which of the following skills is not built with this project?

a. Understanding of various kinds of written expression, including non-alphabetic languages.
b. Building multi-cultural awareness that will increase understanding between students of different backgrounds.
c. Reading for purposes of information or new knowledge (i.e. 'reading to learn').
d. Exposure to various media to build literacy skills across all levels of reading ability.

71. Reading can be best described as:

a. A skill that is learned through sequential lessons and concepts, presented carefully in order of importance.
b. An understanding of the written word.
c. A complex task that involves multiple physical and cognitive processes.
d. The primary form of transmitting knowledge within a culture.

72. Suppose a teacher is helping students categorize animals as carnivores, herbivores, and omnivores using an explanation in a biology text. Which of the following types of exercises will be of most help to students in identifying these categories and their definitions as explained in the text?

a. Summarizing
b. Cloze sentences
c. Creative extension
d. Term memorization

73. Which of the following activities would support a student who is high in Gardner's Logical-Mathematical intelligence type?

a. Writing and giving an oral presentation
b. Designing and utilizing spreadsheets
c. Composing and performing a song
d. A cooperative learning project

74. After students have read the first chapter of a book, their teacher asks them to speculate on what the main character is going to do next. The students are being asked to use a comprehension strategy called:

a. Summarizing
b. Monitoring and correcting
c. Making predictions
d. Drawing conclusions

75. Among the following author purposes for writing literature, which is likely to require the most interpretation on the part of the reader?

a. To inform
b. To entertain
c. To evoke moods
d. To satirize something

76. When summarizing text as part of a comprehension strategy, which of the following is an attribute of a good summary?

a. A summary should be detailed.
b. A summary should be thorough.
c. A summary should mostly consist of main ideas.
d. A summary should repeat the information in a passage.

77. A teacher wants to work on her students' listening comprehension in addition to their reading comprehension since she understands that the skills are interrelated. She has a series of short stories that she thinks the students will enjoy. Which of the following would be the best supplement to typical written comprehension exercises?

a. Preview the content and then read the stories aloud to the students. Assess listening comprehension through verbal and written questions.
b. Ask the students to choose one story each to read aloud to a small group. Encourage the students to discuss what they have learned afterward.
c. Assign each student a story to read and require them to write a report on it. Each student should then present his or her report based on what he or she has learned to the class.
d. Have the students read stories aloud to the class, and create mock tests based upon the main ideas which they identify.

78. Which of the following instructional strategies would likely help students the most in understanding the difference between denotation and connotation and help them learn to identify the connotation of a word in context?

a. Providing example sentences in multiple choice questions asking for a word's connotation
b. Filling out a Venn diagram with sets of words that have connotations, denotations, or both
c. Assigning a reading where students identify and highlight words that have connotations
d. Giving word definitions and asking students to describe the feelings elicited by each definition

79. A teacher is working with a student who is struggling with reading. The teacher gives him a story with key words missing:

> The boy wanted to take the dog for a walk. The boy opened the door. The _____ ran out. The ____ looked for the dog. When he found the dog, he was very ______.

The student is able to fill in the blanks by considering:

a. Syntax. Oftentimes, word order gives enough clues that a reader can predict what happens next.
b. Pretext. By previewing the story, the student can deduce the missing words.
c. Context. By considering the other words in the story, the student can determine the missing words.
d. Sequencing. By putting the ideas in logical order, the student can determine the missing words.

80. A teacher notices that her new student, Carl, has a hard time answering questions related to comprehension during class and has scored low on comprehension quizzes and worksheets. What would be the most logical first step in determining how to help Carl?

a. Encourage Carl to read all assigned texts at least twice before class to help him understand what he has read.
b. Provide Carl with story maps of what he will be reading to assist his comprehension visually.
c. Ask Carl to read aloud with his teacher individually so that she can ensure that he is reading with expected accuracy and speed (i.e., fluently).
d. Modify Carl's class work so that he is able to work on easier comprehension material until his skills are brought up to speed.

81. Which of the following choices shows the correct type of text matched with an appropriate strategy for increasing reading comprehension?

a. Popular magazine: critical analysis/deconstruction
b. Literary novel: key concept synthesis
c. Persuasive essay: journaling over time, recording personal thoughts about the reading
d. Chapter from science textbook: text outlining with vocabulary and main ideas

82. For making speeches, which nonverbal behaviors enhance audience perceptions of speaker credibility?

a. Making eye contact with certain listeners
b. Making random/unrelated body motions
c. Making startling/novel facial expressions
d. Making gestures congruent with meaning

83. What is an accurate reflection of criteria for clear, concise speech presentations?

a. A speaker should not take three or more minutes more to get to the point.
b. A speaker should not pause before answering audience questions.
c. A speaker should include as many anecdotes and details as possible.
d. A speaker should include both necessary and interesting information.

84. Making a strong argument in a speech, conversation, or debate requires:

a. Forceful delivery
b. Acknowledging the opposing point of view with respect
c. Demonstrating the weakness of the opposing view with mockery
d. Seizing the floor when the opponent's point is strong
e. Seizing the floor when the opponent's point is weak

85. Which of the following statements is most true?

a. Introducing oral and written texts from a variety of cultures can enhance students' understanding and appreciation of language.
b. Children typically learn language best when exposed primarily to texts exemplary of their own background or culture, thereby increasing their ability to identify personally with what they are learning.
c. Studying other languages will impair a student's ability to develop his or her own first language.
d. Students should be exposed to one type of text at a time to diminish genre confusion.

86. Which of the following activities would incorporate the best use of technology to increase students' oral language skills?

a. Students visit the school computer lab to work on math and science activities with software that utilizes voice-recognition technology in an interactive process.
b. Students use an internet program and computer camera to converse with English-speaking students in other countries.
c. Students can visit the classroom's Language Lab, in which there are tape recorders and CD players. Students can use these players to listen to novels, poetry, and other literary works on tape.
d. A teacher videotapes a class discussion about a story and replays it for the students to watch and discuss.

87. For a class with half native English-speaking students and half ELL students from various countries, what is the best way the teacher can promote intercultural understanding through reading?

a. Have the native English-speaking students read about other cultures, and have the ELLs read about mainstream culture.
b. Have all students read equal amounts of text that reflect both mainstream and other cultures.
c. Have the native English-speaking students read about mainstream culture, and have ELLs read about their own cultures.
d. Have all of these students choose the cultures they want to read about and the texts to read.

88. Which of the following statements regarding the acquisition of language is FALSE?

a. Young children often have the ability to comprehend written language just as early as they can comprehend or reproduce oral language when given appropriate instruction.
b. Oral language typically develops before a child understands the relationship between spoken and written words.
c. Most young children are first exposed to written language when an adult reads aloud.
d. A child's ability to speak, read, and write depends on a variety of physiological factors, as well as environmental factors.

89. Research indicates that developing oral language proficiency in emergent readers is important because:

a. Proficiency with oral language enhances students' phonemic awareness and increases vocabulary.
b. The more verbally expressive emergent readers are, the more confident they become. Such students will embrace both Academic and Independent reading levels.
c. It encourages curiosity about others. With strong oral language skills, students begin to question the world around them. The more they ask, the richer their background knowledge.
d. It demonstrates to students that their ideas are important and worth sharing.

90. A teacher is instructing students in listening strategies for evaluating the effectiveness of the messages they hear. Which of the following strategies is a bottom-up strategy?

a. Listening to identify the main idea
b. Listening to identify specific details
c. Listening to summarize the content
d. Listening to infer or make predictions

91. Which of these components of speech delivery is most effective for establishing rapport and personal connection with the audience?

a. Eye contact
b. Vocal tones
c. Articulation
d. Movement

92. Public speakers want to give speeches that make their audience pay attention, but they also want to give speeches whose messages are meaningful enough to remain in audience member's minds. This can best be accomplished with:

a. Simple language and stories
b. Strict logical progression
c. Sophisticated language and ideas
d. Eye contact

93. Which of the following statements is true about TV and radio as types of media for communicating ideas?

a. TV is a high-status mass medium, but radio is not.
b. TV does not have as broad of a reach as radio does.
c. TV and radio can both serve to raise awareness.
d. TV targets more specific audiences than radio.

94. Which of the following best develops student oral vocabulary, spoken narrative skills, and connections between spoken and printed language?

a. Correctly spelling, pronouncing, and using new words in telling stories to the class
b. Learning new vocabulary words and spelling them correctly in written narratives
c. Learning new vocabulary words in listening, speaking, and storytelling activities
d. Correctly identifying new vocabulary words in listening and reading exercises

95. Teachers must consider student developmental levels when assigning cooperative learning projects and/or discussions. For example, students are bored by topics at younger age levels and lost by topics at older ones. In addition to chronological age, which other developmental level does this example relate to most?

a. Social developmental levels
b. Cognitive developmental levels
c. Emotional developmental levels
d. Behavioral developmental levels

96. Which of these correctly represents findings about research-based vocabulary instruction?

a. Children need word repetition consisting of drills for vocabulary development.
b. Children need only be exposed to new words once or twice to remember them.
c. Children learn the vocabulary in texts best indirectly through simply reading them.
d. Children require direct instruction and word exposure in various contexts.

97. A middle school ELA teacher wants to avoid assigning traditional homework wherein students must research a topic and report their findings to the class. Instead, she wants to enable students to make more positive connections by responding to stimuli in a web-based tool as homework, which will also stimulate classroom discussion more effectively. Which technology tool would accomplish this best?

a. Blog
b. Podcast
c. RSS feed
d. Videoconference

98. In learning the alphabetic principle, which do children typically develop first?

a. They learn the shapes of letters.
b. They learn the sounds of letters.
c. They learn these all concurrently.
d. They learn the names of letters.

99. Which of the following is accurate regarding conversational vs. academic English for ESL students?

a. Conversational English is not as cognitively demanding of ESL students as academic English.
b. Conversational English deficits are the causes for ESL academic underachievement.
c. Conversational English is harder for ESL students to develop than academic English.
d. Conversational English takes the same time for ESLs to develop as academic English.

100. Following instruction time, Ms. Pitman provides each student with a small sign that can be hung around the waist or neck. Ten children in her class receive signs displaying a single weekly vocabulary word. Five students get signs with the following: *dis-*, *re-*, *pre-*, *un-*, and *mis-*. The remaining students have signs with the following: *-ing*, *-ed*, *-s*, *-less*, and *-ful*. What is the best choice for a follow-up class activity based on this information?

a. The students are arranged into groups to demonstrate tangibly that certain parts of the English language have fixed functions.
b. Each student must use his or her sign to brainstorm a list of possible words that include those letters.
c. Each time a bell is rung, students must find a new partner with whom he or she can combine signs to make a new word.
d. Ask each student to explain what his or her sign means and how it functions in the English language.

Answer Key and Explanations for Test #2

1. C: The main idea can be found in the third sentence of the first paragraph. The first two sentences bring up the subject of helping teachers and giving students an improved educational experience, but the Library Media Center is not mentioned until the third sentence.

2. C: The first sentence of the second paragraph is the best example of a topic sentence as it states the main topic of the paragraph. The first two sentences of the first paragraph (A and B) provide some background for the subject but do not mention the topic. The second sentence in the second paragraph (D) gives details that support that paragraph's topic sentence.

3. B: The word *juggle* here refers to the teacher's need to balance many different responsibilities. While the teacher undoubtedly hopes to succeed, that is not the meaning of the word here. A juggler may waver (C) as he or she tosses (D) balls, but the literal meaning of juggling does not apply here.

4. A: To *augment* something is to increase it or make it greater. While the library may correct some misinformation (A) or change a student's education (C), these are not the meaning of *augment*. "Color" (D) is *pigment*, not *augment*.

5. C: This is the best restatement of the main idea. Choices A and B restate information from the first two sentences, but the main idea is found in the third sentence. Choice D restates a detail from the final paragraph.

6. A: The word *feeble* means weak, infirm, or unable to walk. It can refer to physical or mental frailty. However, when meaning *senile* (B), it is more commonly compounded to *feeble-minded*. The sentence is not referring to memory loss but to weakness in enforcing classroom management. Both *haphazard* (C) and *rare* (D) could fit the context of the sentence, but do not match the meaning of *feeble*.

7. B: The verb *to temper* means to moderate, tone down, or change, whether used literally such as "to temper glass or metal," or figuratively as in "to temper emotion with reason." Its meaning is closest to that of the adjective *temperate*, meaning moderate, such as a temperate climate or disposition, rather than the noun *temper* meaning the heat of anger (A); the noun *temper* meaning one's disposition (C), such as "she has an even temper"; or the adjective *temperamental*, meaning sensitive, moody, or irritable (D). The sentence is explaining that strictness is made more moderate, or balanced, by kindness.

8. C: The main idea that a teacher's classroom management style affects the classroom environment and success of teaching is stated in the last sentence of the first paragraph. The title (A) identifies the topic of classroom management but not the main idea of the four styles. The first sentence of the first paragraph (C) introduces the topic. The last sentence of the last paragraph (D) gives supporting details on one classroom management style.

9. C: The first and third paragraphs begin with a statement that introduces the topic of that paragraph. The second paragraph discusses the four classroom management styles and begins with the first one rather than introducing the topic, so the first sentence of each is not a topic sentence (A). Two paragraphs do have a topic sentence, not just a main idea, so choice B is incorrect. The topic sentences are not at the conclusion of each paragraph (D).

10. D: The first paragraph introduces the topic, briefly describing each of the four classroom management styles. The second paragraph goes into more detail on each style, describing the effect each has on the students and class environment. The final paragraph suggests which style is most effective for positive outcomes. This paragraph is more of an application of previous material than a summary of it (A). No true problem and solution are mentioned (B), and neither are a cause and effect (C).

11. D: Foreshadowing is the best choice. Choice A, first-person point of view, does not answer the question and is incorrect because the story is told from the third-person point of view. Choice B is incorrect because *hyperbole* generally refers to unrealistic exaggeration, but the imagery in this passage is realistic, even if it does describe extreme conditions. Choice C, *onomatopoeia*, is incorrect because the passage contains no words like *cluck* or *quack* that sound like what they describe. Choice D foreshadows the character's eventual fate by hinting at the freezing death in the first paragraph.

12. D: Choice C is close to being the answer, but choice D is the best answer because the narrator can enter the consciousness of both the man and the dog, making it third person omniscient. Choices A and B can be ruled out because the narrator does not use the pronouns *I* or *we*.

13. C: Only interpretation III fits with the meaning of the passage. The narrator's statement that the man lacked imagination means that he did not have the foresight to realize that he was risking his life. Interpretation I is incorrect because the passage reads, "He was quick and alert in the things of life." Interpretation II is incorrect because the quote shows lack of imagination as a danger, not something unneeded.

14. B: There is no indication in the passage that the Bennets are interested in becoming friends with Mr. Bingley (A), that Mr. Bingley would be a valuable business connection (C), or that Mr. Bingley has any prior knowledge of the Bennet daughters (D). Mrs. Bennet tells her husband that a new neighbor is moving in: "Mrs. Long says that Netherfield is taken by a young man of large fortune." Mrs. Bennet is sure he will make an excellent husband for one of her daughters: "You must know that I am thinking of his marrying one of them."

15. B: Mrs. Bennet is exasperated by her husband, meaning that she is frustrated or annoyed and fed up with her husband's seeming indifference to Mr. Bingley: "'My dear Mr. Bennet,' replied his wife, 'how can you be so tiresome!'" Being annoyed would indicate that she is not indifferent toward him. She also is the person who initiated the dialog and seems to eagerly want to talk to him about her ideas. This would indicate that she is neither tired nor afraid of her husband.

16. B: The evidence in this selection indicates that marrying a man with money was a primary goal for young women. Mrs. Bennet tells Mr. Bennet that Mr. Bingley is "A single man of large fortune; four or five thousand a year." Mrs. Bennet further indicates that she is thrilled with the news because of Mr. Bingley's potential as a husband for one of her daughters: "What a fine thing for our girls... You must know that I am thinking of his marrying one of them."

17. A: Mr. Bennet is facetiously asking if the idea of marriage (particularly to one of his own daughters) was Mr. Bingley's intention when he agreed to rent Netherfield Park.

18. C: A stanza consists of a grouping of lines, set off by a space, that usually has a set pattern of meter and rhyme. This poem has six stanzas.

19. D: Personification is a metaphor in which a thing or abstraction is represented as a person. Personification is used to varying degrees throughout the poem, but of the answer choices given, the one that represents Spring as a woman waking from sleep is the best example.

20. A: The previous stanza gives clues as to whom *we* refers:

> "Not one would mind, neither bird nor tree
> If mankind perished utterly"

We is referencing mankind.

21. B: This is an example of a rhymed verse poem. The last two words of each line rhymes in every stanza. A sonnet is a poem of fourteen lines following a set rhyme scheme and logical structure. Often, poets use iambic pentameter when writing sonnets. A free verse poem is written without using strict meter or rhyme. A lyric poem is a short poem that expresses personal feelings, which may or may not be set to music.

22. A: Answer choice A gives the best summary of the poem. The poem imagines nature reclaiming the earth after humanity has been wiped out by a war. The poet imagines how little the human race will be missed.

23. A: The article provides information about a scheme to defraud internet users of money. It describes the mechanics of the fraud scheme and explains how the perpetrators intend to make money.

24. B: A *propensity* is a tendency to do something. Proclivity is a synonym for this. *Larceny* is a synonym for theft. Note that *pilferage* and *robbery* are also synonyms for theft, but that *talent,* which is a latent ability, does not mean the same thing as propensity, while *disinclination* has the opposite meaning.

25. D: Despite what might seem the unlikely nature of the come-on, according to the text the Nigerian letter scheme succeeds in bilking people out of millions of dollars annually.

26. C: Choice C is correct because reporting findings from case studies is a rhetorical means of providing evidence to support purposes, viewpoints, or claims in informational text. Choice A is incorrect because relating personal anecdotes is a rhetorical means of appealing to reader emotions and making points more relatable or accessible to readers, but not of providing evidence. Choice B is incorrect because making analogies to clarify ideas is a rhetorical means of explaining by helping readers connect ideas in the text to knowledge they already have. Choice D is incorrect because laying out premises and conclusions provides a logical argument based on deductive reasoning, but it does not provide evidence.

27. D: First the writer should narrow down all potential topics to a main idea. Then he or she should identify main points supporting that main idea, decide how to sequence those main points (B), list all the details that support each of the main points (A), and then organize those details in a logical, effective order (C).

28. C: The first step the reader should take for evaluating argumentative writing is to identify what assumptions the author has made about the issue s/he discusses in the writing. Assumptions are things that the author accepts without proof. If an author's assumptions are incorrect or illogical, the ensuing argument will be flawed. Readers can be misled by argumentative writing if they do not identify the author's assumptions. The reader's second step is to identify what kinds of evidence the author has offered to support the argument (D). The reader should then take the third step of evaluating how relevant this evidence is (B). The fourth step for the reader is to evaluate how objective the author is about the issue discussed in the writing (A).

29. D: Explaining a process to readers (A), articulating a concept for readers (B), and presenting new information to readers (C) are all primary functions of informative or explanatory writing. Proving a point to convince readers to agree with the author's position (D) is a primary function of argumentative writing.

30. C: Mnemonic devices help with remembering key sets of information by organizing it into patterns. For example, many mnemonic devices are made by identifying a series of initial letters corresponding to the words that must be remembered but forming an easily remembered acronym or phrase using the same initial letters (such as "RAFT" or "Role, Audience, Format, Topic" to help students remember the key elements of a writing assignment). The other answer choices reflect devices that are useful for reading and writing but are not specifically used for remembering key sets of information. Making outlines (A) helps with identifying main ideas and supporting details and organizing them into a hierarchy. Checklists (B) help ensure one has completed all steps or components of a task or project. Graphic organizers (D) help with visually representing abstract concepts and relationships.

31. C: Outlining provides a structure that is based on the main point and supporting details, and writers often use outlines to plan the order in which these will be discussed in the composition. Therefore, choice C is correct. Choice A is incorrect because outlining helps the writer visualize the sequence of supporting details, not necessarily the relationships between supporting details. Choice B is incorrect because outlining is used by writers at all levels. Choice D is incorrect because outlining typically requires at the most a single sentence to summarize any given point.

32. B: If a researcher finds too little material about a research question, s/he should broaden the question, which may be too narrow to yield enough literature. If there is an unmanageable, seemingly unlimited amount of literature, s/he likely needs to narrow, not broaden the research question because it is too general. Many people voluntarily doing research enjoy information and can get overwhelmed by all the data they find. Knowing the research question in advance can keep the wealth of information from impeding progress. On new topics, sometimes no research literature exists yet. This does not mean that no type of searching helps: doing systematic searches can help, for example, first through periodical abstracts to get an overview of literature related to the topic, then through references cited in specific sources like individual research papers, and/or references cited in general sources like books about specific related topics.

33. B: When teachers assign cooperative writing partnerships, each student in a pair should not always take only one role (A); they must both take turns writing and reviewing their partner's writing (B) to experience both roles in the process. Each student should provide not only positive feedback (C) or only constructive feedback (D) to a partner, but both. For example, if the assignment is using descriptive adjectives, positive feedback would be identifying specific descriptive adjectives the partner used; constructive feedback could be identifying sentences that could use more descriptive adjectives.

34. C: Setting clear goals, observing concrete data, and applying learning are all aspects of inquiry strategies, so choice C is correct. Each of the other choices refers to a teaching approach or set of strategies that does not involve these elements. Prewriting strategies (A) include helping students generate ideas, organize ideas, access their background knowledge, identify research topics, and use graphics to visualize ideas. Modeling strategies (B) includes teacher demonstration, giving students exemplary models of expected writing types, helping students analyze models, and inviting students to emulate effective model elements in their writing. Process writing (D) includes giving students opportunities for extended practice, peer interaction, personal responsibility, writing for authentic audiences, and self-evaluation.

35. B: Studies show that cooperative learning is an effective practice for teaching many things, including writing (A). Experts recommend that when assigning cooperative writing partners or groups, teachers provide students with both a structure (C), and explicit expectations (D) for both partnership/group and individual performance.

36. C: Writing instruction strategies proven effective by multiple research studies include brainstorming to plan before writing; explicit instruction of students by teachers in techniques for planning, revising, and editing compositions; explicit instruction in steps to follow for writing argumentation; collaborative work among students to plan, write, edit, and revise their writing in groups; and teacher modeling of writing strategies. Of these, teacher modeling should be introduced initially and then gradually faded as students gain experience and confidence with practice until they independently apply the strategies consistently.

37. A: An introduction should move from broad, general statements about a topic to a focused and specific point regarding the topic. This point is the thesis statement. While the strongest points should come later in the body of an essay, the most attention-grabbing statements should be those in the introduction, as these will serve to engage the reader's interest in the topic and in reading the rest of the essay. Therefore, choice B is incorrect. Starting with focused and specific statements followed by broad and general statements is the opposite of how an introduction should be structured, so choice C is incorrect. Writing experts advise that the technique of beginning an essay with a dictionary definition has become overused and should therefore be avoided, so choice D is incorrect.

38. B: How appropriate the content of a student's composition is reflects function rather than form. Composition length (A), word usage (C), and spelling (D) in a student's composition are all reflections of the composition's form rather than its function.

39. A: Both similes and metaphors make comparisons, but not in the same way. A simile uses words such as like or as, while a metaphor discards these words, usually referring to one thing as another to show what they have in common, such as referring to a crowd as "a sea of faces" to show how large it is.

40. A: Prefixes and suffixes are important for reading comprehension because they change the meanings of the root word to which they are attached. A student who understands that *un* means "not" will be able to decipher the meanings of words such as *unwanted, unhappy,* or *unreasonable.*

41. A: Directions for installation are the most likely of the choices to contain the word "you," particularly as the reader of the text should be personally following the instructions given (i.e. "You will next remove the orange cap to access the tank."). (b) and (c) would both be more likely to use the first-person pronoun "I" than the second-person "you". (d) is more likely to contain the third-person pronoun "we."

42. A: Repetition—of words, phrases, sounds, images, or ideas—and appeal to sentiment are both effective tools of persuasion. Repetition causes consumers to better recall information, regardless of their response to the message itself. Appeal to sentiment taps into consumers' emotions, making consumers more likely to engage with the content. Choice B is incorrect because "weasel words" that qualify claims tend to be needed for overstated claims rather than understated ones. Choice C is incorrect because advertising uses humor to persuade more often than news or advocacy. Choice D is incorrect because hyperbole, superlatives, and intensifiers are used frequently across the advertising world and do not reflect anything about the quality of the advertising content in which they are used.

43. D: The purpose of narrative writing (A) is to entertain readers with a story. Even when authors want to offer insights or teach lessons while entertaining readers, they accomplish this through storytelling. The purpose of expository writing (B) is to inform or direct readers. The purpose of persuasive writing (C) is to convince readers to agree with the author's position or argument. The purpose of speculative writing (D) is to encourage readers to explore ideas and potential responses rather than entertain, tell stories, inform, explain, direct, or convince.

44. D: The passage directly states that *Beowulf* is important because "it is often viewed as the first significant work of English literature," making D the correct answer choice.

45. C: Proving that something is factual, accurate, or true is typically what a writer of argumentative or persuasive writing does. Writers of explanatory writing, in contrast, will assume that something is factual, accurate, and true and then analyze, explain, and clarify this information to help readers understand it. This explanation can include differentiating among members of a given category; defining certain terms; analyzing or breaking down processes into their stages, phases, steps, or components; and/or developing concepts for the reading audience. Argumentative writing works to convince readers that something is so; explanatory writing works to explain why something is so.

46. C: Among the choices, only choice C seems unlikely to be helpful in character analysis. In order to understand a literary character and analyze his or her development, readers should keep a few things in mind. One element to pay close attention to is the observations the narrator makes about a character, as the author likely has a reason for including these in the work (A). The reader can also observe contradictions in what a character thinks, says, and does, as these may reveal internal conflict and may play a role in the character's development (B). Additionally, readers can note differences between how the other characters in the story talk about a character and how the narrator talks about the character. This can reveal facts about the character's relationships with other characters, for example, and reveal how aware a character is of their own behavior or qualities.

47. B: Comprehension is a process of creating meaning from that which a student reads, sees, hears, or experiences. The tools for comprehending are similar across genres. The teacher has specifically chosen a passage and wants the students to compare, not contrast, the pieces. Dickensian writing is not generally considered to be journalistic, as suggested in Choice "a". Choice "c" is correct—you can in fact compare even unlike things. However, Choice "b" provides a richer backdrop for showing students how to link that which they read in school to their own lives and use the same tools to comprehend and take meaning from whatever they read.

48. B: This finding, if true, most directly supports the student's claim that literature has a profound impact on society and individuals. It provides empirical evidence that reading literature with diverse characters and experiences can lead to increased empathy and tolerance in individuals, demonstrating how literature can shape attitudes and behaviors. This aligns with the student's argument that literature can evoke empathy and influence perceptions.

49. C: These features are most characteristic of traditional literature, which has been adapted by authors from oral traditions including folklore, epics, fables, proverbs, and fairy tales. The modern fantasy (A) genre, which includes modern-day fairy tales and tells imaginative tales, may use traditional literature themes as its foundation but is original writing by authors such as Hans Christian Andersen, Lewis Carroll, and E.B. White. Picture books (B) combine text and pictures, which help beginning students learn to read by supplementing words with illustrations. Poetry books (D) contain poems rather than prose writing.

50. C: Poems are typically the most condensed or economical in their use of words. Plays (A), typically more condensed in language than novels because more of the story is told directly through actions which novels must verbally describe, are still not as condensed as poems because they contain more dialogue. Novels (B) are full-length books, by definition longer than short stories, novelettes, or novellas; they often elaborate more about plot and character development than many poems, thus using more words. They also more often use complete sentences throughout, whereas poems may use phrases in addition to/instead of sentences. Essays (D) tend to expound on nonfictional topics in prose; hence, although they are far shorter than novels, they use many more words to express ideas than plays or most poems.

51. D: Virginia Woolf had a powerful effect on the modern novel. Other authors that influenced the Modernist movement include T. S. Eliot, Ezra Pound, James Joyce, and Gertrude Stein. The Modernist movement took place in the late 19th and early 20th centuries. The authors questioned traditional forms of literature and in doing so, wrote novels and poems that were full of modern thought.

52. B: The mood of a literary work establishes the emotional atmosphere through the author's use of setting, details, imagery, objects, and words. One example is a mood of mystery. Tone is the author's implied or stated attitude toward the subject matter of the work. For example, the author might create a humorous, joyous, bitter, ironic, earnest, serious, optimistic, or pessimistic tone through the use of details and word choice. For instance, a work's setting or a character might have a mysterious mood, but be treated with a humorous or ironic tone. Conflict is a literary element that provides the basis for a plot. Examples of generalized conflicts include man versus nature, man versus society, man versus man, or man versus self. Point of view is the literary element of who tells the story, such as a first person, third-person objective, third-person limited, or omniscient narrator.

53. B: Fantasy stories and books revolve around magical or supernatural creatures. Science fiction is a similar genre, but it relies on the portrayal of a future world, creatures from other planets or galaxies, etc. The action and adventure genre typically involves heroic characters in dangerous and exciting scenarios, such as solving a mystery or journeying through an unfamiliar environment. Historical fiction stories are set sometime in the past and are usually accurate in their historical information.

54. B: The *roman à clef*, or "novel with a key," tells a story that readers cannot fully understand without the "key," which explains some elements and details. The purpose is to disguise truths that are too threatening to state explicitly, so choice B is correct. Choice A is incorrect because the purpose is not to challenge readers, and choice C is incorrect because the purpose is not to deliberately confuse readers; both of these purposes run contrary to one of the main motivations of writing in the first place—to communicate. Writing of painful personal experiences (even in disguise) can give authors catharsis, but the purpose of the *roman à clef* is not to create distance between these experiences and the reader, but to express these disturbing realities without inflicting the same trauma on the reader, so choice D is incorrect.

55. D: Teachers are expected to give students plenty of opportunities not only to read different literary genres independently (A), but also to listen to literature read aloud (B), to attend or view productions of dramatic literature, to express their responses to literature in writing and speech (C), and to interact with others (D) in class and group discussions, pairs, cooperative learning projects, conversations, etc.

56. C: William Shakespeare's plays are good literary examples of poetry within fictional drama because they are written in verse form. Poems typically do not contain inserted prose (A). Plays are not generally known to incorporate pieces of fictional prose (B). Nonfictional prose sometimes incorporates quotations of poetry or even occasionally original poems, but this occurs much less often than with Shakespeare's plays and many others written entirely or mostly in poetry (D).

57. D: Historical fiction is set during some previous period of our history, which may be remote, recent, or anything in between; science fiction is set during the possible future (A) or during an imagined alternative present—either one with scientific, social, and other developments not part of current reality. Historical fiction is based on periods, events, and facts from history; science fiction is based on speculations (B) of what may occur through extending current science. However, both forms can be concerned with events occurring around and/or to the characters and inventions (real and/or imaginary) could also be included in either one (C).

58. C: Although both subgenres are fiction, they are not always about fictional *characters* (a): some tell fictional *stories* about *real* characters—e.g., Anthony Burgess's novel *Nothing Like the Sun* about what he imagined as Shakespeare's life, or Mary Renault's *The Bull from the Sea* about her conception of Theseus (apparently historical figure and myth combined) and the Minotaur. Similarly, other historical and science fiction may contain only fictional characters' fictional individual experiences, but within actual events—e.g., Esther Forbes' novel *Johnny Tremain*, set before and during the American Revolution. Thomas Pynchon's historical novel *Against the Day*; science fiction novels *Earth* by David Brin, *Callahan's Key* by Spider Robinson, *The Astronauts* by Stanislaw Lem; and many others were based on a 1908 explosion (probably from a meteorite or comet) in Tunguska, Siberia. Numerous other examples exist. Some historical and science fiction works are closely aligned with facts; others are far more imaginative (d). Because they are ultimately fiction, both involve some kind of speculation (c).

59. B: The division described in the question is termed a *stanza* in poetry. A verse (A) is a single line rather than a group of lines, as far as poetry is concerned—though in songs it is a group of lines, like a stanza in a poem. A refrain (C) is a verse, set of verses, or set of words that is repeated regularly throughout a ballad, other poem, or song. A paragraph (D) is like a stanza in that it expresses a group of related ideas and it is separate from other paragraphs. However, it is used in prose, not in poetry.

60. B: When students work in pairs to read and identify parts of an informational text to aid their comprehension, they read portions silently, discuss and agree on what they believe to be the main idea, and then identify details that would support that idea. This process is best summarized by choice B, so it is the correct answer. Identifying genres is not always necessary for comprehension, so choice A is incorrect. While prior knowledge is a consideration in the reading of informational text, a paired reading exercise to aid in comprehension need not involve the students identifying their shared prior knowledge, so choice C is incorrect. Identifying external texts that support the author's view may be necessary as part of research for a paper, but it is not necessary for understanding an informational text, so choice D is incorrect.

61. C: Class composition and preferences. Before selecting literature for the classroom, the teacher needs to assess the class, considering where they are with their reading skills and what their current interests are. After determining these things, the teacher would next evaluate books that seem appropriate for this particular group of children in terms of plot, character, and reading level.

62. D: These books by Jane Yolen and Beverly Cleary are fantasies that are written for children who read at a typical second-grade level. The books included in choices A and B are too difficult for second-grade students. The titles in choice C are good examples of realistic fiction.

63. D: The denouement is the end of a story. The other choices are intermediate steps in writing a story.

64. A: Descriptive writing uses many sensory details to paint a vivid picture of a scene, character, event, etc. so that readers can imagine they are actually experiencing it firsthand. Hence identifying sensory details in an entirely descriptive passage is the most helpful of these strategies. Retelling (B) is a better strategy for comprehension of a narrative passage that includes some plot, action(s), and/or event(s) but would help less with a passage lacking these. Previewing (C) the passage would help students who have already learned to identify sensory details, but if they do not know to look for these, previewing would be less helpful than teaching them to do so. Self-monitoring (D) is a metacognitive strategy useful for reading comprehension, but it can apply to so many different reading behaviors that it is not as specific to the descriptive passage as identifying sensory details. Students may self-monitor to ensure they are identifying sensory details in descriptive writing, but they still must learn to identify them first.

65. B: The intention of round robin reading is to provide practice reading aloud with appropriate fluency. This practice is also used to cover a large quantity of text with the entire class during the class period. By pairing the students, each child will get more practice reading aloud. He or she will also be more likely to stay engaged when working with only one partner, as there will be less time and fewer opportunities to become distracted. The teacher can then circulate amongst the groups to encourage focus and concentration, as well as provide guidance on fluency and comprehension of the text. As long as the students are paired carefully, this strategy is most likely preferable to the round robin method.

66. C: The teacher is involving them in the concept of faith through Bonhoeffer's life. A is incorrect because details of World War II are not discussed.

B is incorrect because details of Germany are not discussed. D is incorrect because the teacher is not primarily providing a multicultural true story.

67. D: Credibility is related to how believable readers felt the author's writing was, which is a major element of whether the author's appeals changed the readers' minds. Clarity, another criterion for evaluating methods of appeal, is related to how clearly the author presented the content. Accuracy, an additional criterion, is related to whether the content that the author included was factually correct. Cohesion, also an evaluative criterion, has to do with how well the author's arguments and appeals are connected and related to one another, which helps readers understand them and holds their interest.

68. C: The author is hoping to persuade or convince readers to either request a pet and/or the primary care of their pet by providing them with facts as well as by using rhetorical devices such as dispelling opposing arguments.

69. B: Reading fluency refers to the speed, inflection and accuracy with which students read, either orally or silently. In order to read fluently, students must be able to decode, or break down into segments, words that adhere to the common rules of the English alphabet. For those words that are generally not easily decoded, students must build their vocabulary of "sight words," which should be recognized without the need to decode. In (A), students may or may not be reading fluently or accurately, since the computer program does not monitor how the student reads. In (C), keyboarding practice bears no direct relationship to reading fluency. In (D), again, the computer is simply a source for text, but does not build any specific fluency skill. In (B), students are exposed to sight words and vocabulary in a fun way. Using a computer program allows for an unlimited supply of relevant words and for accurate scoring.

70. B: Mrs. Taylor's project introduces students to an ancient form of expression that was written, but not based upon alphabetic principles, like English. This project is applicable to all levels of readers, as it incorporates various kinds of media to assist comprehension. Students are required to listen and read for information so that they can apply what they have learned to creating their own hieroglyphics. In Choice B, the answer suggests that what is learned about hieroglyphics will assist students in understanding those with different backgrounds. However, hieroglyphics are not used in any widespread way today, and are much less helpful in building multicultural awareness than perhaps a lesson on modern Egyptian culture or writing.

71. C: Reading is a process that involves several physical and neurological processes. In order to read, an individual must employ the use of his or her body to access and physically see the written words. The brain must then use schemata to decode or recognize the words and determine their meaning. Often, a reader uses prior knowledge and deductive reasoning to understand the meaning of non-literal text. The skills necessary to read evolve simultaneously and cannot necessarily be taught in exactly the same way for each person. A reader engages in both understanding *and* creating meaning from a text.

72. B: Cloze sentences are sentences with certain words or phrases from a given text replaced with blanks. They allow students to fill in the blanks and thereby use a reasoning process to learn the meanings of terms. This type of activity would be the most effective of those listed in the other answer choices for helping students understand the text and the terms it presents, so choice B is correct. Summarizing may be helpful, but it would not target specific terms, as cloze sentences would, so choice A is incorrect. Creative extension would help in applying the concepts one they are learned, but it would not be possible until the concepts are learned, so choice C is incorrect. Rote memorization would not enable students to use reasoning, so it would not necessarily be an aid to understanding the text or the terms, so choice D is incorrect.

73. B: In his Multiple Intelligences theory, Howard Gardner defines the Logical-Mathematical intelligence type as the ability to identify symbolic, numerical, and logical forms and patterns. A teacher could support a student high in this intelligence by assigning activities like designing and utilizing spreadsheets, organizing and analyzing data, and making estimates and predictions. Writing and giving an oral presentation is an activity that would support a student high in Gardner's Verbal-Linguistic intelligence type, who excels in spoken and written language and verbal communication. Composing and performing a song is an activity that would support a student high in Gardner's Musical-Rhythmic intelligence, as that student can appreciate and/or produce music and rhythms. A cooperative learning project is an activity that would support a student high in Gardner's Interpersonal intelligence type, who can detect and understand others' emotions and interacts well with others.

74. C: Predicting events in a story builds anticipation and helps propel the reading forward. Students activate prior knowledge from life and literature to understand characters and anticipate their thoughts and actions.

75. D: When the purpose is to inform (choice A), readers know because most or all of the text provides facts, explains reasons, or gives procedural directions. Readers recognize entertainment (choice B) when they are amused by descriptions and dialogue, excited by action, perplexed by mystery, or in such suspense to discover what happens they cannot put down the text. Readers recognize evoking moods (choice C) in word choices connoting sadness, fear, elation, etc. Satire (choice D) requires more interpretation; for example, in the essay "A Modest Proposal," Jonathan Swift wrote in a deadpan tone, as if he was seriously suggesting cannibalism as an economic and social solution, to lampoon English society.

76. C: A good summary of text captures the main ideas, omitting the details and other less important information. A summary does not literally retell the text or repeat it word for word. It shows reader comprehension by paraphrasing the major meaning of the text in the reader's own words.

77. A: In (A), the teacher guides previewing of information to show students how to put themselves in the right frame of mind to listen carefully for meaning. Students are then able to listen in a guided way based upon the previewing. By varying the type of comprehension assessment, the teacher will get a better understanding of what the students learned. (B) is a good exercise but does not provide for direct instruction by the teacher or a particularly skilled student. In (C), students are focusing more on reading comprehension than listening since they must read the story to themselves and then write a report. There is then no way to gauge what they have learned. (D) would be useful but does not include teacher-guided previewing, which is very helpful in building comprehension.

78. A: An effective way to teach students the difference between denotation and connotation is to provide example sentences and have students choose a given word that best expresses the connotation of a highlighted word in each sentence. For example, to show the connotation of the word *challenge*, an example sentence "This is one of the many challenges that must be faced in order to solve the problem" could be given, and students could choose whether the connotation suggested by "challenges" in this case was "threats," "obstacles," "criticisms," or "setbacks." This instructional strategy is summarized in choice A, which is the correct answer. Since words generally have denotations and may or may not have connotations depending on their use, a Venn diagram would be misleading, and choice B is incorrect. Choice C is also incorrect, as highlighting words in a passage would not require students to distinguish between denotations and connotations, nor even to identify the exact connotations of words in context. Choice D would not be logical, since not all words have an emotional connotation, and the definition alone will be of little use for determining the connotations of a specific use of a word.

79. C: By considering the other words in the story, the student can determine the missing words. The student is depending on the information supplied by the rest of the story. This information puts the story into context.

80. C: Many factors can affect a student's ability to understand what he or she is reading. Building comprehension skills is an ongoing process and can be made difficult if a student lacks the appropriate level of reading fluency. If he or she cannot read accurately or with enough speed, he or she will have much more trouble with comprehension than the average student. It is important to identify any decoding or vocabulary problems that might be affecting comprehension first; if those can be solved, comprehension skills may naturally increase as reading fluency increases.

81. D: When students read textual information for another subject, they are expected to pick out important words and concepts and retain them. By outlining the text, the student can keep track of the overall framework of information, as well as word definitions and main ideas. In Choice "a", the primary purpose for reading is likely entertainment. In Choice "b", a more appropriate reading comprehension strategy would not focus on key concepts at the expense of the literary style and tools. In Choice "c", it would be correct to analyze a persuasive essay for main ideas and supportive evidence, rather than an extended free-writing exercise.

82. D: Nonverbal behaviors during speeches influence the listeners' perceptions of the speaker's competence, good character, trustworthiness, and therefore credibility. Speakers should make eye contact with everybody in the audience, not just certain listeners (A). Their body movements should not be random or unrelated (B) to what they are saying (e.g., pacing, face rubbing, playing with one's hair, tapping pencils or toes, etc.), but they should reinforce their verbal messages. Facial expressions should not be startling or unexpected (C); they should be consistent with both the verbal content and the speaker's vocal tones. A speaker's gestures should also be congruent with the meaning (D) of what s/he is saying, to fit with and emphasize the points they are communicating.

83. A: When a speaker is making a statement or answering a question from the audience, s/he should not take three or more minutes to get to the point, which will lose listener attention. Getting off the subject has the same effect. However, speakers should not be afraid to pause before answering audience questions (B): this gives them time to formulate a clear response, as well as demonstrating to their listeners that they are thoughtful and in control. Including too many anecdotes and details (C) is not good: it causes audiences to lose track of the subject/get confused. Similarly, speakers should include necessary information but not all other interesting information. (D): Information overload triggers listeners' brains to shut down due to having more input than they can process.

84. B: A strong argument is not made by forcing people to pay attention, interrupting another speaker, or belittling an idea, person, or group. These behaviors simply weaken the speaker's position because they each demonstrate in a different way that the speaker is not in control of his own ideas, and must therefore try to control the situation by using emotion. The most successful arguments acknowledge the strongest points of the opposition, and then unemotionally dissect those points in order to find and demonstrate how they are flawed.

85. A: Students are completely capable of understanding and appreciating oral traditions and written texts from other world cultures, as well as those originating from cultures in the students' own community. In fact, introducing a variety of material can increase some students' appreciation of language and literature as it enables them to learn about the world around them. Language skills emerge at a point in most children's development during which students are fascinated with learning new concepts. Introducing a variety of texts also benefits students in a classroom who belong to other cultures; these students are able to learn concepts from texts that represent their family, culture, or country of origin.

86. B: Oral language skills incorporate speaking, listening, and knowledge of conventional language. In choice A, students would be limited to a very specific vocabulary in order to work with the science and math programs, and would not have opportunities to increase their knowledge of language. In choice C, students are practicing their listening skills, but are not required to speak or think critically about what they have heard. Choice D does involve technology and class discussions; however, the benefit of watching the discussion on tape is relatively unclear. In choice B, students not only have a chance to build their speaking and listening skills, but also increase their knowledge of other cultures and ways of speaking.

87. B: The best way to promote intercultural understanding among students through reading is to have all students read equal amounts of text reflecting the mainstream culture and the other cultures from which the ELL students come. Option (A) would certainly expose all students to cultures other than their own, but it would not enable all students to read about both mainstream and other cultures. Option (C) would not expose either student group to cultures other than their own. Though it is important to give students some choice in reading materials, leaving text selection entirely up to students (D) cannot ensure variety or balance, let alone equity, and also deprives students of teacher guidance in selecting reading matter.

88. A: Most adults can understand the relationship between oral and written language: components of oral language have representational symbols that can be written and decoded. However, most normally-developing children acquire spoken language first and begin to develop reading and writing skills as they approach school-age. Many children are first exposed to the concept of written language when an adult introduces books or other written texts. However, a child's ability to read and write develops over time and is dependent on the development of physiological processes such as hearing, sight, and fine motor skills for writing. Written language development also typically requires direct instruction. Most children must be taught to read and write and rarely learn these skills simply by observing others.

89. A: Proficiency with oral language enhances students' phonemic awareness and increases vocabulary. Understanding that words are scripted with specific letters representing specific sounds is essential to decoding a text. Students cannot effectively learn to read without the ability to decode. An enhanced vocabulary supports the act of reading; the larger an emergent reader's vocabulary, the more quickly he will learn to read. He will be able to decode more words, which he can organize into word families and use to decode unfamiliar words.

90. B: Bottom-up listening strategies are text-based: listeners ascertain meaning from the language used in the text by listening to identify specific details, syntactic patterns, cognates, etc. Top-down listening strategies are listener-based: listeners activate their own background knowledge of the subject matter, context, situation, text genre or type, and language used to ascertain the main idea (A) in the text; to be able to summarize its content (C); and to interpret text by making inferences and predicting (D) what may come next.

91. A: Speakers can establish rapport and personal connection with audiences by making eye contact with the audience. Vocal tones (B) can be used to express enthusiasm, emphasize important points, and maintain audience attention, but it is not the most effective among these choices for building rapport. Articulation (C) is important for ensuring audience comprehension, but it is not as important as eye contact for building rapport. Similarly, body movement (D) is less crucial for rapport than eye contact is, though it is still important for emphasizing messages and maintaining the audience's attention.

92. A: Audience members are most likely to retain the points of a speech or lecture if they are offered in the form of a story and the speaker uses language that is simple and direct enough to be transparent. The stories need to be simple, and must drive the speech directly toward an essential and clear point. Including anecdotes is most effective when the speaker uses storytelling techniques that will bring them alive, such as varying pace, pitch, and intensity, using body language to suggest a change in speakers, and using the stage to suggest a setting.

93. C: Choice C is correct because both TV and radio can raise awareness, interest, and excitement. Choice A is incorrect because both TV and radio are high-status mass media (i.e., they reach many people). Choice B is incorrect, as TV has a broad reach and radio has a broad-to-medium reach.

Choice D is incorrect because, while TV enables messages to be targeted for certain audiences, radio works better for specific audiences, such as people who listen to a particular local station every day.

94. A: Learning correct spelling and pronunciation of new vocabulary words develops student connections between spoken and printed language; using the new words in telling stories to the class develops student spoken narrative skills. Option B develops vocabulary and written language skills but not necessarily oral vocabulary. It also does not address spoken narrative skills or spoken-printed language connections. Option C develops oral language and narrative skills but does not address spoken-printed language connections. Option D addresses receptive vocabulary recognition and receptive connections between spoken and printed language but not expressive oral vocabulary, expressive spoken-printed language production, or spoken narrative skills.

95. B: The topics of cooperative projects and/or discussions and whether they are age-appropriate in difficulty relate most to cognitive developmental levels, i.e., what they can understand. Social developmental levels (A) relate to whether students can interact effectively in peer groups. Emotional developmental levels (C) relate to student emotional intelligence, i.e., emotional self-management plus sensitivity to, understanding of, and appropriate response to others' emotions. Behavioral developmental levels (D) relate to whether students can regulate their behaviors appropriately within peer groups.

96. D: Research-based vocabulary instruction findings show that children need ample word repetition, but not through drilling. Multiple exposures to the same words in different contexts are more effective. Multiple and repeated exposures are important because children do not learn vocabulary through only one or two exposures to a new word. Research finds that they do not simply learn vocabulary in texts indirectly from reading; instead, teachers must give them direct instruction in the new vocabulary words they find in their texts.

97. A: Students can post, read, and comment on blog posts at home and in school, facilitating homework and classroom discussion. Podcasts (B) can stimulate dialogues between their creators and viewers, but as download files, they preclude dynamic interactions such as class discussions. RSS feeds (C) are good for students/teachers to read teachers'/other students' posts, but they are typically unilateral, not permitting interactive discussion online. Videoconference (D) does enable online communication, but only in real time, and content is not easy to retrieve or saved automatically.

98. D: The alphabetic principle is the concept that printed letters and letter combinations correspond to speech sounds. Children often first become familiar with the names of letters, which supports later learning of the sounds they represent. First they learn letter names, then they learn the shapes of the letters (A), and then they learn the sounds indicated by the letters (B). Although there can be some overlap, children typically know more letter names before they fully learn all letter shapes and sounds (C).

99. A: Conversational English is much *less* difficult (A) for ESL students to learn because it is much less demanding of them cognitively. Most often, academic underachievement in ESL students is caused by deficits in academic, not conversational English (B). The disparity in ease of developing these separate skill sets—basic, everyday-life interpersonal communication skills in conversational English vs. the complex-compound syntax and vocabularies specific to math, science, social studies, and other content areas in academic English—is apparent in the fact that while most ESL children develop conversational English within about two years of living in English-speaking settings, they take at least five to seven years to develop academic English (D).

100. C: One-half of the class receives signs showing vocabulary words, which are probably used as root words. The remaining students are split into two general groups: those with prefixes on their signs and those with suffixes. The best approach is to get the students moving, listening, and talking in order to solidify their understanding of how roots, suffixes, and prefixes work together to make new meanings out of various root words. This approach also allows the students to participate in a game in a group context, making the activity more fun and engaging.